Manual to the sociology of the school

Manual to the sociology of the school

Royston Lambert
Spencer Millham Roger Bullock

Dartington Research Unit in the Sociology of Education

Weidenfeld and Nicolson
5 Winsley Street London W1

ISBN 0 297 17828 8

Reproduced and Printed in Great Britain by
Redwood Press Limited, Trowbridge & London

Contents

Preface

This book is the first publication of the Dartington Research Unit into the Sociology of Education. It presents an analytic structure and a methodology by which to study a school or a similar educational institution. The theoretical framework and practical methods were developed and tested in a study of boarding and day schools, the empirical reports on which are being published separately. It will be one function of the Dartington Research Unit to apply and develop further this analytic structure by the study of a whole range of educational institutions or particular aspects of them. The unit is, at the moment, applying it in a study of twenty schools for young offenders in this country.

This book has been a collaborative effort over several years. My co-authors, Roger Bullock and Spencer Millham, contributed greatly in both matter and production, and we cannot disentangle our respective contributions. At an earlier stage Susan Stagg helped considerably with several sections and the whole has benefited from discussions with several others on my former research staff, especially Penelope FitzGerald and Raymond Woolfe. Geoffrey Hawthorn of the University of Essex also gave valuable criticism.

Carol Haine typed early drafts, but the brunt of a complex manuscript in various versions has been indomitably borne by Mrs Pullen and Aileen Stein.

The research, of which this book is one report, was financed by the Department of Education and Science, and housed by my former colleagues, the Provost and Fellows of King's College, in their Research Centre.

I am deeply grateful to them all.

Royston Lambert,
Dartington Hall School,
Totnes, Devon.

Introduction

1

This book is intended as a guide, a manual of reference or of departure for the study of a school or educational institution. It provides a set of concepts and hypotheses, a detailed sociological framework of analysis, a tested group of methods and a bibliography as a set of working tools and measures for anyone who wishes to examine the social structure and dynamic operation of a school or a similar institution as a small ongoing society. The sociological model of a school, definitions and methods presented here have been evolved during five years of intensive research into schools as organisations covering a hundred day and boarding schools. Over the years the sociological approaches have all been continuously modified in the light of theoretical reformulation, empirical results and experience in the field. They now comprise serviceable instruments which can be applied to day or residential schools or colleges of any kind. Still more diverse uses will suggest yet more modifications, a sharpening of concepts, a refinement and extension of the model and its typologies, and an elaboration of the methodology. This manual does not claim to be the perfected, immutable end of a study, but a beginning, an attempt at a navigational chart and set of implements which sum up past exploration, and guide yet further ventures into this rewarding new branch of the sociology of education.

Until recently the sociology of education in this country, insofar as it existed at all as a separate branch of study, was little concerned with the school as an organisation. It tended to see the school either in terms of its functions for the society in general, or in terms of the primary units of which it was composed. As far as general society went, the school was seen principally as a mechanism of *allocation*, by which society trains, socialises, recruits members of its various strata, occupations or groupings. The school was studied primarily as an agency of social mobility, and the relationship between the general (tripartite) system of schools, internal mechanisms of allocation such as selection at the age of eleven or streaming, and the class system and intelligence distribution of society have been a chief preoccupation of educational sociology in England since the war. Partly as a result of major empirical studies such as those of Halsey and Floud, Douglas and Ross or Jackson, on class, intelligence and social mobility and allocation through the school system, fundamental changes of educational policy are taking place which attempt to reduce the influence of social class differences on schools as allocative systems and thus to extend opportunities of education and social mobility by eliminating premature selection or rigorous ' streaming '. Alongside this major and largely British theme of study, there have been some significant studies of the internal constituents of the school or college which derive from the pioneering work of Parsons on the school class, Moreno on sociometry, Coleman on pupil culture, Sanford on college culture, and others in the United States. There have been valuable studies of teachers as groups, of the teacher's role, of culture conflict within the school, of the classroom unit and its roles, and of the informal grouping of pupils. But neither these studies of the school's primary constituents, nor those which related some of its functions to the macrocosm have generated a theory or empirical framework by which the school can be understood and explored as a coherent and distinct social organisation in its own right.

Recently such a development has been occurring as a result of impulses from within the sociology of education and from other branches of the science. There has been a growing interest in the school's function as an *integrative* mechanism for society, as a means of socialisation of the young, of training (as well as allocation) for adolescent and adult roles, and of transmission of the culture of society, its values, norms and their accepted modes of expression and renewal. To understand how these functions are performed, it is necessary to look at the whole structure and interlocking and dynamic operation of the society of the school, as well as its relationships with outside organisations, cultures and parasystems. The important work of Professor Bernstein on communication is thus set in the context of a study of schools as ongoing societies differing from each other and in their relations with the cultural background of their pupils.

Another impulse has come from the study of organisations of

quite other kinds. From the classic studies of the 1930s in the United States, of industrial or administrative units, a theory of 'organisational sociology' has been evolved covering the goals, structure and operation of such specific social constructs serving given goals. More recently, other organisations, not serving the clear end of producing inanimate objects, have been examined from the theoretical standpoint, concepts and methodology of organisational sociology. Starting with prisons in an early study by Clemmer, other custodial or semi-custodial institutions have been extensively studied. But the application of organisational theory and analysis has been much less noticeable in the field of education, whether in school or higher educational institutions, residential or day. One reason for this may be that, though schools and the like are specific social constructions as much as a factory or mental hospital, the goals which they serve are more diffuse and impalpable and their means of control are less utilitarian or all-pervasive. Whatever the reasons, we still have no organisational theory of the school, and until recently, no systematic model or profile to aid organisational analysis. But recent work in various universities —among them London, Manchester, Essex, York and Keele, and the work of this research unit—indicates that this approach to the study of the school is beginning to bear fruit, and promises to enlarge the sociology of education and enrich our knowledge of the educational process.*

How? What does the study of the school as an organisation have to offer the teacher, the sociologist or the administrator? In substance it takes us to the heart of the educational process because it is concerned with the institutional methods by which transmission of values, training in roles and preparation for society are attained. It enables us to examine each or all of those methods either as embodied in a formal structure or as developed in less formal personal interactions. It relates the various elements of the formal structures and processes of institutions to the informal life which operates within them, and thus permits us to see how the whole or the part promotes, deflects, or prevents the attainment of differing educational and institutional ends. In method, it offers objectivity of approach, not only in the sense of value-free indices and techniques, but also in the sense of a coherent body of concepts

* Since this was written a valuable general introduction to the *Sociology of the School* has appeared by M. Shipman, Longmans, 1968.

and perspectives, which, tested and developed by subsequent research, accumulates into a valid theory of this kind of organisation. Finally, the organisational approach enables comparison to be made objectively *between* schools, either in terms of their individual elements or their performance as operating wholes. To sum up in less sociological language, if we wish to know what ends our schools and colleges suppose themselves to serve, the structures, methods and dynamics by which these ends are realised or otherwise, and if we wish to do this objectively and make comparisons between institutions, then we have to study the school as an organisation.

2   The school as an organisation

How then does a school appear in the light of organisational sociology? Differing perspectives might stress different elements, but here we briefly single out the elements which are crucial to any conception of the school as a small society, leaving the reader to follow the details and subsidiary issues through the sociological framework of a school which forms the main part of this book. Precise definitions of the sociological terms used in this introduction will be found below on pp. 41–44.

The school or institution is conceived as an organisation or social system constructed to attain specific goals and defined by its own boundaries and boundary maintaining devices from other organisations or social units which impinge upon it. Though the presenting culture of its members (that is, the culture of family units, peer groupings, the pupils' society, that of the staff and the neighbourhood), and the demands of the wider systems which it serves (educational policy, university or occupational requirements, the L E A administrative structure) inevitably condition its structure and working, the school practically and analytically still operates as a social system in its own right. The use of the word 'system' should not mislead the reader into supposing that this analysis is of the structural-functional variety of sociological explanation, which conceives the society as a sort of organic unity or 'system' like the human body, with its constituent parts functioning harmoniously to maintain the equilibrium and continued operation of the whole. On the contrary, the analysis of the school in the main part of this book should be interpreted always in the light of potential or actual conflict between the constituent elements of the society. Such conflicts produce a continuous dynamic disequilibrium which may promote, divert or frustrate the attainment of ends, may induce change or pressures for change and thus may transform the society, transfix it, maintain its development or bring about its collapse. It is in this perspective of in-built conflict that the chief elements of the school as an organisation should be viewed.*

(i) Goals Unlike a factory, where production is a paramount aim, or a mental hospital, where therapeutic ends are dominant (however important other aims such as the well-being of the members are in both places), a school has goals which are more diffuse. Its goals, the state of affairs which the society exists to attain or promote, fall into three analytic categories: (a) *instrumental goals*, those concerned with the transmission of skills or socially useful attributes, e.g. 'O' levels, physique, manual or verbal or social skills; (b) *expressive goals*, those concerned with the transmission of values or culture or development of the personality regardless of social usefulness, e.g. religion, moral guidance, self-expression in the arts, 'sportsmanship'; and (c) *organisational goals*, those which are concerned with the maintenance of the school as an ongoing society, e.g. the level of discipline and order, routine, recruitment, reputation. In practice, these goals can be combined. Thus, religion in a school serves instrumental ends, by imparting factual knowledge and textual skills; expressive ones, by transmitting values and moral awareness, and organisational ones, by being used to dignify corporate consciousness, or even as a means of control or administration. All schools pursue these three kinds of goal, though individual schools and groups of schools differ in the degree to which they pursue each. Boarding schools, for example, tend to be more concerned with expressive goals than day schools. These differences of emphasis, which are fairly easy to distinguish by research, are

* Although this manual combines functional and conflict models, a third sociological approach should not be neglected. This is a *developmental* approach, which emphasises the ways in which the organisation has changed or developed over a period of time. Obviously influences from the past do have an important part in determining the nature of the organisation.

crucial to any comparative study of schools as societies. Within one school, however, the goals are not static: there is a tension between all three kinds. Organisational goals (e.g. preoccupation with the school's reputation, with a high level of order, or mechanical devices, such as rigid streaming) have a tendency to displace the others, particularly expressive ones; while between expressive and instrumental goals there is a latent conflict, which may be increased by the pressures of the parasystem or of the presenting culture – in the way external examinations, for example, induced over-specialisation. Endemic conflict between these goals is a chief dynamic of the school society.

Not only the intrinsic nature of goals, but the degree to which they are perceived and ranked by differing members of the society and outsiders affect its structure and operation. Goals are not objective entities: they exist only in people's perceptions of them. To outside organisations and its parasystems, the school authorities may present a body of *stated goals*, but these may differ in order of priority from the *real goals* which, in day to day practice, are actually pursued. Thus the school authorities may put prime among its stated aims ' self-expression through the arts ', but in its daily timetabling, routine, specialisation and facilities may allow this goal but little scope. Individuals and the groups into which they fall may likewise interpret or rank the schools goals in different ways; for example, the Old Boys or Governing Body may rank the schools goals differently from the head, the staff may differ among themselves on the priority of instrumental, expressive and organisational ends, and, not infrequently, pupils accept instrumental ends as primary while staff give priority to expressive ones. Again, such varying perceptions profoundly affect the operation of schools, the degree to which they attain or fall short of their different ends, and provide an inherent conflict situation and momentum.

Finally, the goals which schools pursue are not always consciously chosen. They are the result of a complex of pressures which bear on the school from outside and within. Historical forces, the pressure of other organisations, the influences which result from the backgrounds of governors, staff and pupils (' the presenting culture') and the functions which the school serves for the wider society, all shape its goals, as much as the educational philosophy or ideals of its members. How much more powerful than educational ideals these external forces can sometimes be was shown in the famous case of Risinghill Comprehensive School, London, where a headmaster attempted radically to change the goals and methods of his school but was frustrated by pressure from other organisations, the presenting culture of most staff and pupils, and by the rigid concept of the historical role and functions of a school in a slum area which many people, outside and inside the school, possessed. The internal processes of the society, as the rest of this book unfolds, and as the case of Risinghill again illustrates, also exercise a profound influence on the goals which are said to be pursued, which actually are pursued, which are falling into abeyance or rising into prominence.

Unreal and theoretical as any such analysis of abstract ' goals ' may seem in the concrete society of a school, it is the fundamental point of departure for subsequent study of the school's operation and structure in whole or part, or of any comparison between individual schools or groupings of them.

(ii) The formal social order In the attainment of goals, the school is articulated into a formal social order.* The chief elements of this we now review briefly; a more thorough analysis and discussion of their interlocking occurs in the next part of this book. To pursue complex and differing ends, the society allocates itself into subdivisions or *subsystems*. Chief among these are the academic, the economic, the athletic, the social, the secretarial or bureaucratic, the domestic, and in some schools, subsystems of living, medical or pastoral care, and extra curricular activity. Such subsystems contain the elements of a miniature society in them-

---

* In this book we use the term ' order ' rather than ' system ' when referring to the official and unofficial social organisation of the school. To talk of a ' formal system ' or an ' informal system ' would, we feel, give the impression of a separate organic entity, functioning to maintain its own equilibrium and perhaps somewhat static. Actual social entities such as the formal and informal groupings and processes in schools do not operate like that. They are subject to growth and decay, imbalance and conflict of aims and parts, unexpected and damaging obstruction of functions, and are intimately linked with the operation and fate of other entities. The word ' order ' is not ideal, but it implies an articulated pattern of social interaction without the static and misleading organic implications of the concept ' system '.

selves; they serve specific goals, are ordered into their own system of roles and control, hierarchies of status and authority, may possess separate professional or domestic personnel, physical plant or recognised territories and modes of communication, and generate their own norms, values and culture. This could be true, of, for example, the academic/teaching subsystem, the form, house or tutor system, or that for games, or the bursarial department, that for feeding or cleaning, or even such relatively small subsystems of some schools such as the library or the sanatorium. Subsystems can profitably be studied as entities in themselves, though such analysis can be unreal: the main personnel of different subsystems (for example, the academic, the athletic, or the pastoral) can often be the same: it is the roles they play that differ. In any discussion of ' the school' as a whole, however, one should never forget the sharply differing subsystems of which it is composed.

Crucial to the society as a whole is the way these subsystems integrate with each other. Inside each one and between each other they generate conflicts which profoundly affect the balance, changing stress on goals and functioning of the society. The patterns by which they *integrate* and the modes of *communication* by which they interlink are thus vital. In the succeeding section of this book some typologies of integration and systems of communication are suggested.

Other integrative elements knit together and articulate the society of the school. For all members (governors, staff, pupils and others) there will be a more or less elaborate process of *assimilation*: by which the newcomer is introduced to the operating goals, the values of the society, and also the role or roles he is expected to play. To maintain a consensus on ends and means, all members of the school society, adults or pupils, are subject to a process of *control*. The controls used in schools differ greatly in their kind, as the analytic framework of this book explains. Different kinds of control profoundly affect the performance of roles, and thereby help to condition the operation of a school over time and the fundamental differences which appear between schools. A knowledge of the prevailing kinds of control within the society is essential to an understanding of its effectiveness in whole or part in attaining its goals. Related to the system or systems of control there will be one or more patterns of *authority*, an order by which decision-making and sanction-giving roles are distributed, legitimated and operated. Linked to this there will be the system of *status*, by which respect and recognition is formally accorded to roles or persons, and this may be rewarded by a complementary system of *privilege*. Authority, status and privilege systems once again vary in their elements, their distribution over subsystems, and relation to other sociological elements, constituting another dynamic or conflicting factor within systems and a differentiating factor between them. As part of its system of control or values the school will possess mechanisms for maintaining its own identity from other organisations or outside units, *boundary maintaining* mechanisms, and these differ between schools, and are related to goals and the structural elements we have introduced.

As part of, or as means to its ends, the society generates a *cultural* system, a range of approved *values* of behaviour, thought, expression, a range of *norms* of conduct or relationships by which these values are put into practice, of *cultural activities*, *traditions* and *rituals* by which values are expressed, symbolised or dignified. Each of these constituents can be explored in its own right, though most fruitfully in relation to the goal and control systems of the society.

So much, then, for the formal social order. This brief outline of it should not leave the reader with the impression that organisational sociology is concerned with such anatomical description. A society, such as a school, is not a corpse. It is in distinguishing the elements of the society, and, above all, *the operating patterns of their interrelationship*, that the value of this approach lies. This is particularly true of the next area of the school society.

(iii) The informal social order Within the framework of the formally prescribed social order, there exist relationships, norms and values not so prescribed by the goals of the society: they constitute the informal social order. Though in this section, and later in our detailed examination of the school society, we treat this informal social pattern as distinct from the formally laid down one, this is purely for analytical purposes. In practice and in theory as related variables, the formal and informal social orders interweave and interact in the individual's and the group's playing of roles, acceptance of norms, and so on. Nevertheless, the degree of integration between the two can vary, and this variation, we find, is one of the key variables between schools, and profoundly conditions the nature and working of the whole school society.

At both adult and pupil level in the society, the elements of the formal social order are repeated in the informal social network which operates within it. Just as there are formal subdivisions, there may be informal ones, ordained by patterns of association or norms or traditions which originate in the private world of staff and pupils. Likewise, the informal order possesses its own methods of communication, processes of assimilation, social controls wielded, systems of status and elites, distribution of power and privilege, and a whole underculture with its own norms, values, prescribed relationships, modes of expression, traditions and rituals. It is possible to trace such systems for all groups in the society, staff, governors, teaching staff, domestic and bureaucratic staff and pupils.

But it is the relationship between the formal order and the informal network which is fundamental. To what degree do they coincide? Does the pattern of formal authority or status (among staff or pupils) correspond with the informal distribution of effective power and status? Does the informal network of communication supplement, supersede or obstruct that which is formally laid down? Do the norms, values and underculture of staff or pupils correspond with the norms, values and culture prescribed officially? Does the pattern of relationships between the pupils or between staff and pupils, prescribed by such norms and enforced by the subtle controls of the informal world, vary from that presented and enforced by the official order? By thus establishing the degree of distance of the two in detail, it is possible to go on and assess the *orientation* of the various informal orders of the school (pupils or staff) to the official ends and formal order, in whole or part, and to assess the degree of *integration* between the formal and informal orders in general, the *scope* of the informal order, and *the degree of consensus* which prevails among its members. Models of these basic interrelationships are suggested later in this book.

Though presented abstractly here, the relationship between these two variables is, in practice, vital to the operating effectiveness of schools in realising their ends and basic to any comparison between them.

Linking the formal and informal orders are two other constituents of the society which deserve separate introduction here:

(iv) Roles The role system is that point where personality and the social system meet: the legitimately expected behaviour of persons in the society. Round this basic sociological element, the society, formal and informal, is constructed. To analyse the distribution of roles in the society (staff and pupils), their complexity and relationship to instrumental, expressive or organisational goals, the degree to which they are formally or informally prescribed and defined is fundamental to the understanding of the formal and informal orders described above and their interaction. As pupil roles and staff roles vary in distribution and relationship to goals between schools, this area of analysis is essential to a comparative approach.

Equally important are the conflicts generated by roles, for these are the basic conflicts in the substructure of the whole society. From these stem, or upon them impinge, all other conflicts within the society: they provide a vital and incessant dynamic for proper functioning or otherwise and for change within the society. Our subsequent analysis outlines the four basic kinds of role conflict found in schools and modes of their resolution.

(v) Change Linking all aspects of the society as it operates from day to day is the process of change. Change in a society takes several forms: changes in real goals, changes in institutional structure, and those which involve no structural alteration. It is necessary to distinguish these three kinds of change from each other, and the direction of change, whether towards or away from the instrumental, expressive and organisational ends of the society. Given such an approach, we can compare the degree and direction of change between schools.* Change is the outcome of a process, and the pressures for and against it, from both in and outside the society, can be ascertained along with the mechanisms for achieving it, the speed by which various kinds of change can be accomplished, and the effects of change on the role structure – effects which powerfully condition the whole process of change itself. Change links

* For an attempt at this as applied to boarding schools see R. Lambert, J. Hipkin, S. Stagg, *New Wine in Old Bottles*, G. Bell & Son, 1969 p. 74.

each part of this sociological analysis and the whole system of the school to the external parasystems in which it exists.

(vi) Adaptation One measure of the effect of the school in attaining its ends is the pupils' adaptation to the goals and their institutionalised means. Our typologies develop the paradigm of adaptation put forward by R. K. Merton in this respect: conformity, ritualism, retreatism, innovation, and rebellion. These responses can be related to the differing instrumental, expressive and organisational goals and areas of the society, and to the nature and orientation of the informal social order. Each can be examined in its incidence over the society and in the degree to which it is held by individuals. In this way we obtain another comparable measure between schools, and between the goal and structural elements within one school. At this point we begin to leave the sociology of an organisation for its social psychology.

So much, then, for an outline of the school as an organisation, a diagram of which appears opposite. In this introduction we have introduced a few elements which later will be further defined, expanded and interconnected. The latter is the key word. This introductory delineation of the school society has inevitably been static, but sociology is concerned to discover and to posit dynamic and valid relationships between different variables. For this reason, at points in the analysis which follows we interconnect the various sociological elements. For example, we suggest that in schools with a certain pattern of goals, particular kinds of control are likely to operate. Similarly, where some kinds of control are prominent then the pupils' adaptations fall into a certain pattern, and their informal society exhibits certain characteristics and outlooks. At the end of the analysis, we suggest a whole range of hypotheses which interlink the various elements which have previously been discussed separately. And finally, by way of illustration, we take the basic unit of all schools, the classroom unit, and to it apply the foregoing analysis. We examine its goals, its systems of control, the roles which may operate within it, patterns of interaction, association and adaptation. We indicate how certain prevailing goals or types of control affect in different ways the other elements, and the whole process and effectiveness of the class in question. It is with such relationships in mind that this introduction should be read and the substance of this book should be used.

THE SCHOOL AS A SOCIAL SYSTEM

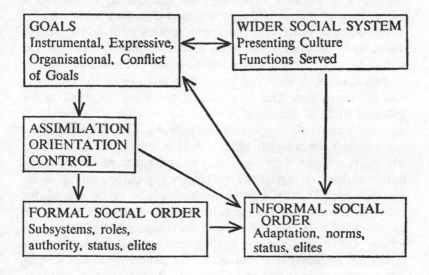

3 **Using this book**

This book arises from research in the field. At the outset of our work we constructed an empirical and theoretical model of the school as a guideline and programme for the researcher in one school and as a means of systematic and objective comparison between schools. As the research proceeded, the model, both its sociological and more empirical parts, underwent drastic revision in the light of concrete experience in the field. For example, the section on authority originally covered solely the distribution of authority among officers. As our research went on, however, it became clear that the *nature* of authority differed significantly between schools, and so new dimensions were developed, on the nature, scope and span of authority, which have proved more useful for analysing and comparing authority in schools. Another example is the fourfold typology of relationship between the formal and informal social orders (p. 128). This relationship has proved to be one of the most important differences between schools, and a vital factor within each. At first we expressed the relationship in a dimenson of six features but, in the light of our fieldwork, have reduced it to the four found on page 129. Similar changes have taken place in the methodology which is discussed below.

The analytic framework presented is thus both empirical and theoretical: there are sections on mundane matters like size and staff-pupil ratios, as well as theoretical models of normative control or role conflict. We do not regret this mixture of the empirical and the theoretical. This is a manual for those interested in the practical study of the school, and we try to relate the concepts to relevant means of discovering, recognising and recording their embodiments. Sociologists often speak of a need for a closer relationship between theory and empiricism, yet some theory seems purely abstract or logical and yet empirically unrecognisable or indeterminable. That is why in presenting our typologies of, for example, informal norms or goal perception, we provide methods to determine what they actually are in the concrete hurly-burly of the school. Of course, we are not contending that theory ('meta-theory') is undesirable or useless, but for the non-specialist sociologist, it can be misleading and alienating. We do contend, however, that observers must have some knowledge of what they are looking for, what to look at, and a programme by which to organise their perceptions and methods. That is what this manual hopes to provide.

The approach provided is that of an analytic framework; it is a theory of the general, or programme or meta-type, which furnishes concepts, typologies and definitions to facilitate the analysis of the school as an organisation. We do not always seek to provide theoretical propositions which link the various elements of the framework into valid or testable relationships. For example, we do not say that when the balance between the types of real goals is XYZ, then the relationship between the formal and informal systems will be type C; or when role conflict type 3 occurs among the staff and prefects, staff-pupil relations will be of kind 2, and the authority system among the pupils of type 4. The sociology of the school as an organisation is too young to be able to produce interrelated hypotheses of this kind which are valid for individual schools and between schools of different kinds. We do, however, provide for the purposes of discussion some hypotheses linking sectors of the analysis which we are testing in our own research. Some sections of the analysis itself (those on the crucial areas of goals, roles, control, the relationship between the formal and informal systems and change) discuss dynamic interrelationships. In general, however, we delineate the separate features of the school as an organisation and leave the user of this manual to connect them together into testable relationships in the concrete situation he is exploring. We stress again, however, that it is when the elements of our framework are so dynamically interconnected that the sociology of an ongoing society begins.

What uses has this book for the sociology or education student, the researcher or whoever is concerned to explore and compare schools as societies? In the middle of study or fieldwork into one aspect of the school, this framework enables its whole structure and operation to be kept in view. We have found it, both in fieldwork and in later analysis, invaluable as a guide and programme which relates our detailed empirical and theoretical pre-occupations to each other and to all other relevant parts of the complex society of the school. Equally, this framework aids the process of objective analysis and comparison. Objectivity lies not so much in the value-freedom of the observer, as in the use of defined and published concepts and methods which can be re-used by others to refine the framework and correct the hypotheses derived from them.*

Part Two, on the social system of the school, is laid out thus. On the *left hand side* there is a written text, explaining the sociological analysis, providing definitions, elucidations, cross-references to the methodology section, and a bibliography. This can be read continuously. Opposite, on the *right hand page*, is a summary or model of the sociological analysis. Once familiar with the content, the user can see at a glance from the right hand pages the salient features of the school society and relate them quickly to whatever he is doing or to each other.

The research from which the manual draws is concerned with boarding as well as day education, and so features of residential schools occur throughout, and are applicable to college or other kinds of residential institutions as well. Residential schools con-

---

* One kind of value judgement remains: e.g. what level of institutional control implies a ' total ' as opposed to a ' non-total ' institution, or when does a ' simple ' role become a ' complex ' one. But this is a different kind of value judgement from a moral evaluation of, for example, what goals are or are not desirable.

tain all the basic features of day schools however, and this framework, with omissions, is fully applicable to the day school. The book does *not*, however, contain the results of our research into boarding and day schools. Anyone who wishes to see the theoretical analysis provided here applied in practice to a group of schools should consult the main report on our substantive findings.*

It is central to the purpose of this book to relate the theoretical analysis of the school to practical methods of validating such theory, of gathering data and exploring concrete situations. At the end of each chapter of the analysis, we therefore discuss the best means of applying and testing it. We give not only a bibliography, but paged references to questions in the interviews and questionnaires, to scales and tests which appear in Part Three, Methodology, of this book. How, for example, does one go about studying control in a school? At the end of the analytical chapter on control, we refer the reader to objective scales in the methodology which help to express the level of control in a school by a numerical score, to interview and questionnaire items which establish its nature, to tests which reveal the kind of informal control used by the pupils, and so on. On p. 251 we provide a table which relates each part of the sociological analysis of the school to the specific questions or methods for obtaining information on the matter which appears later in the book. The methodological part of the book is also laid out, with a commentary between each item or question, so that it can be read and studied in its own right.

One major caution should be made about this methodology. The methods which suit one piece of research or study may not suit another. Each methodology is designed to test certain hypotheses, and as the hypotheses which govern each piece of research will differ, so must the methods used. The interviews, scales, tests and questionnaires given here obviously cannot simply be applied wholesale to another piece of research or study. They are methods which *we* have found useful for our purposes, after much piloting, reshaping, research and subsequent analysis. They are certainly not the *only* methods, or infallible or final ones. We offer them as practical guides to action, which the user, in his own study or research, can consider, adopt, alter, or reject. Our subsequent re-

---

* *Boarding Education: a sociological study*, to be published by Weidenfeld and Nicolson.

port on our empirical finding will show the use we have made of them.*

Indeed, it is in this tentative spirit that we publish this manual. The sociology of the school as an organisation is not mature enough for us to offer finite hypotheses or concepts or methods. Inevitably, some areas of our framework are at a more advanced theoretical level than others. There are many other approaches to the sociology of the school which remain to be explored. This book is a beginning not an end. We expect and hope that the framework it provides, the definitions, concepts and methods, will be continually scrutinised, refined, adapted and improved. We hope to keep the *Manual* up to date with such criticisms and developments, and with relevant literature. But we believe that it fulfils a purpose now in linking empirical and theoretical approaches, providing an overall framework and specific typologies by which schools can be examined and compared. It is because we, and others, have found it a valuable catalyst, and because the fruits of studying the school as an organisation are so great, that we venture to print it.

4 General Bibliography

The following texts are relevant to general *organisation theory:*
V. Aubert 1968; P. M. Blau 1963; A. Etzioni 1961, 1962; M. Friedell 1967; M. Haire 1959; J. G. March 1965; R. Mayntz 1964; P. Mouzelis 1966; R. K. Merton 1951; T. Parsons 1951, 1960, 1961.

The following texts are relevant to an organisation theory of the school:
R. G. Barker 1963; H. S. Becker 1961; W. A. L. Blyth 1965; R. Bullock 1967; J. A. M. Davies 1957; J. H. Fichter 1962; J. Floud 1961; C. W. Gordon 1957; E. Hoyle 1965; G. E. Jensen 1954; H. Jones 1965; R. J. Lambert 1966; J. D. R. MacConnell 1967; P. L. Masters 1966; T. W. G. Miller 1961; T. M. Newcomb 1967; J. Partridge 1966; R. Pedley 1963; M. Punch 1966; G. Rose 1967; N. Sandford 1962; M. Shipman 1968; F. M. Stevens 1960; D. Street 1966; W. Taylor 1963; W. Waller 1932; J. Webb 1962; I. Weinberg 1967; J. Wilson 1967.

* *Ibid.* See also Lambert, Hipkin and Stagg, *New Wine in Old Bottles.*

The following studies of other types of institution may be relevant to certain sections of the framework:
B. Bettelheim 1961; K. Brill 1964; G. W. Brown 1962; W. Caudill 1958; D. Clemmer 1958; D. Cressey 1961; S. M. Dornbusch 1955; R. Giallombardo 1966; A. Giddens 1960; E. Goffman 1961; D. L. Howard 1960; T. Morris 1963; H. W. Polsky 1962; M. E. Spiro 1958; M. Stanton 1954; G. Sykes 1958; D. A. Ward 1965; W. F. Whyte 1955.

In case of joint authorship the name of the first author is given. Details of the publications may be found in the bibliography at the end of the manual.

Part one

Preliminary factual data about the school

We start with a summary of basic factual data about the secondary school. It is an important section should a quick classification of schools by some basic differences be required.

Most information for this section is easily obtained from the prospectus, interviews and school lists, although it is necessary to cross-check such information; for example, the size of the school as stated in a list or prospectus may differ from the numbers on the termly lists, and there are frequent changes in timetable, subject choices and extracurricular activities.

Usually the sections are self-explanatory, as they deal with descriptive details, but a comment is added where confusion may arise.

1. NAME OF SCHOOL ....

2. TYPE OF SCHOOL (CONSTITUTIONALLY)

L E A maintained	1
Voluntary Aided/Controlled	2
Direct Grant	3
Independent Progressive	4
Independent non-H M C	5
Independent H M C	6

The category 'Independent Progressive' covers a group of schools which are members of the so-called Co-educational Conference. Details of the schools are given in H. Child's *The Independent Progressive School*, Hutchinson, 1962.

HMC refers to schools in membership of the Headmasters' Conference.

3. OWNERSHIP

Public (Trust, Governors, L E A)	1
Private (Private Trust)	2
Private (Profit)	3

This section attempts to distinguish three types of ownership. In two, the school is owned by a non-profit making trust (one public, one private) and the third occurs where the school is run as a private concern for profit (usually the headmaster will be owner).

4. ACADEMIC GRADING

Grammar or similar	1
Technical	2
Bilateral	3
Comprehensive	4
Secondary Modern	5

5. SEX COMPOSITION

Boys only	1
Girls only	2
Mixed	3

6. AGE OF ENTRY

At any age below 11	1
All at 11	2
All at 13	3

All over 13	4
Some 11, some 13	5
Some 13, some 16	6
At any age above 11	7

7. TIME OF ENTRY

All at beginning of year	1
All termly	2
At any time	3

8. APPLICATION AND PLACES AVAILABLE

                                                      Boys   Girls

Number of places available last September:
Number of applicants considered for each
of these places:

9. SCHOOLS ATTENDED PREVIOUSLY

1 Separate junior department
2 Primary schools
3 Preparatory schools
% leavers from junior dept entering upper school
% of senior school from junior dept
% of senior school from other main feeding schools

10. BOARDING COMPOSITION

                                                      Boys   Girls

Number of boarders
% of school who are boarders

B

11. SIZE OF MAIN OR SENIOR SCHOOL

Boys   Girls

Total number of pupils in main or senior school
Total number of pupils doing post 'O' level
(excluding 'O' level repeats) courses
% of pupils doing post 'O' level (excluding 'O'
level repeats) courses

12. BASIC SOCIAL SUBUNITS

Number

Form (as a social unit)
Tutor group (as a social unit)
House
Junior-Middle-Senior Blocks (Age Groups)
Other
Most schools are subdivided into social units for administration, control, pastoral care, etc.

13. MEANS OF DIVISION OF SUBUNITS

Horizontal Division
Vertical Division
If vertical, add details of any further subdivision into broad age groups, which are kept distinct or remain attached to house:

   (i)   *junior-middle/senior*
  (ii)   *junior/middle-senior*
 (iii)   *junior/middle/senior*

The social divisions may be horizontal (i.e. same age groups) or vertical (i.e. across age groups) or both. The vertical groups may be further subdivided in some schools into separate age groups, for example, juniors may be kept separate from the rest, or seniors from the rest. Thus in certain comprehensives there are upper, middle, lower schools which are separate for most organisational purposes.

14. FEES

No fees: L E A maintained
Fees for boarders: £————— per annum
Fees for day pupils: £—————per annum
Give details of presence and numbers of pupils who are:
(i) *Full fee paying: boarding and tuition*
(ii) *Full boarding fees but not tuition*
(iii) *Boarding fees only on a means scale*
(iv) *Free places*
(v) *Total supported to some degree by*
    L E A's *(known to school)*
Much information here can be obtained from an interview with the headmaster or bursar (see p. 298). In residential schools the total number of pupils who get help with fees from L E A S or a charitable trust is a rough guide to the proportion with officially recognised need for residential education (e.g. parents abroad, isolated home, family disturbance, vocational training). Occasionally parents receive such assistance direct, so the school's estimate can be an underestimate.

15. GEOGRAPHICAL REGION

The geographical location of the school
A classification of geographical areas has to be drawn up for the purpose. The one used in our survey simply classified by groups of counties on north, south, east, west, midlands, etc. basis.

16. LOCATION OF SCHOOL

In centre of large town	1
In suburb of large town	2
In country town	3
In village	4
Isolated in countryside	5

The more sociologically relevant details of school location (such as class of neighbourhood, catchment area), are analysed in the chapter on 'The school in the wider social setting'. (pp. 193–208).

17. DENOMINATION

Give denomination of school (if any): ————————————
It must be remembered that many independent and some state schools are denominational foundations and prefer most (not all) of their pupils to belong to that church. For most state schools, obviously there is usually no laid down denomination. Again the more sociologically relevant aspects, for example, the religious affiliations of the parents and staff, are analysed in the chapter on 'The school in the wider social setting'.

18. STAFF

(i) Number of teaching (classroom teaching) staff excluding headmaster
Full time:———————   Part time:———————
(ii) Staff-Pupil Ratio:
Crude:———————   Weighted:———————
The staff-pupil ratio is easily calculated.
The crude ratio is obtained by dividing the number of pupils by the number of staff, counting a part timer who does classroom teaching as one-tenth of a full time teacher for each half-day taught.

The weighted ratio takes into account the extra staff needed for 'A' level and other work where groups are smaller. The weighting can vary. The one used here counted all pupils doing post 'O' level (excluding 'O' level repeats) work twice and proceeded as before. Another example of a weighting system can be found in G. Kalton, *The Public Schools*, Longmans, 1966.

If boarding school

	Resident in school	Non-resident
(iii) Number of housemasters		
Number of assistant housemasters		
Number of house matrons		
Number of others who help in running the house		
Specify the roles of the non-teaching staff involved in running the house		

In residential schools, the other roles of non-teaching staff are important. Some schools for example have house mothers or use matrons or staff wives to a great degree.

(iv) *Staff turnover:*

    (a) Number of teaching staff who left school (for any reason) last July: ——————

    % of teaching staff who left school (for any reason) last July: ——————

    (b) Number of teaching staff who have joined school in last 3 years: ——————

    % of teaching staff who have joined school in last 3 years: ——————

    (c) Turnover of other boarding staff who are not teachers:

Part two

The school as a social system

1. Introduction

From this summary of basic data we now turn to the sociological analysis of the school as a social system by looking at the overall structure and its operation. Throughout, the emphasis is on the sociological aspects of the school rather than descriptive detail. Because of this, some empirical aspects of the school or its environment which are often considered as categories in their own right—parents, for example, or the private world of the staff—are in this analysis distributed according to their relevance to basic sociological features: the goals of schools, roles, authority, and so on. In this way parents, for example, who may indirectly influence goals, appear in the chapter on goals (chapter I), but, as they also act as a pressure for change, they appear in chapter VI on change whilst other aspects of their education and class occur in the chapter on the school and the wider social setting (chapter VIII). If this arrangement is kept in mind, the following analysis should present no difficulty to non-sociologists who are more used to thinking of social groups such as ' teachers ' and ' pupils ' rather than of the social structure in which they interact. In the last chapter, on the classroom unit, one major empirical area of the school society is discussed according to the whole sociological analysis which has been used in this part of the book.

2. Definitions

We start with definitions of the terms we use in the analysis (they are repeated later in each of the chapters to which they relate). Below are the definitions of terms which will recur throughout the book. The definitions given are devised by us. Some need exposition in separate papers, most could be further refined, but some interim definitions are necessary if a social system is to be analysed. These are working tools, not final sociological statements.

(*i*) *Authority:* Institutionalised power over others which is considered legitimate by those over whom authority is wielded and by the formal social order.

(*ii*) *Control:* Mechanisms for maintenance of consensus on value orientations; or by which motivation is kept at a level, and in the direction, necessary for the continuing of the operation of the social system towards its ends.

(*iii*) *Culture:* A system of beliefs, value orientations and expressive symbols.

(*iv*) *Custodial:* Maintaining separation, directly and indirectly, from influences outside the institution which threaten its instrumental, expressive or organisational goals. (This reverses the usual definition of *custodial* by which the outside world is protected from the inmates.)

(*v*) *Deviance:* Failure to conform to institutionalised norms.

(*vi*) *Dysfunction:* The effect of a social phenomenon or institution in impairing the maintenance of or preventing some condition or trend in the wider social systems of which it is a part.

(*vii*) *Elite:* A high status group which is self-selecting and self-perpetuating.

(*viii*) *Expressive:* That which is an end in itself (although it may have instrumental functions), that which satisfies the need dispositions of the performer as distinct from the performance, the technical operations or processes necessary to attain such satisfaction.

(*ix*) *Formal Social Order:* Norms, values and relationships prescribed structurally or normatively by the goal system.

(x) Function:	The effect of a social phenomenon or institution in maintaining or promoting some condition or trend in the wider social systems of which it is a part.*
(xi) Goal:	The state of affairs which the society exists to attain or promote.
(xii) Informal Social Order:	Norms, values and relationships not prescribed structurally or normatively by the goal system but which may have functions for it.
(xiii) Instrumental:	That which is a means to a further end, that which appertains to performance in the sense of necessary technical operations rather than the satisfaction induced by performance or by the attainment of the end of the performance.
(xiv) Need-disposition:	A tendency to fulfil some requirement of the organism, a tendency to accomplish some end state, a disposition to do something with an object designed to accomplish this end state.
(xv) Norm:	A common standard which guides and defines the limits of members' responses in an established group.
(xvi) Organisational:	That which maintains an ongoing social system.
(xvii) Power:	An actor's ability to induce or influence another actor to carry out his directives or any other norms he supports.
(xviii) Real Goal:	The state of affairs to which the resources and activities of the society are immediately directed (this can be a long-term goal, a means to it, or a goal which is distinct from long-term ones).
(xix) Role:	The legitimately expected behaviour of persons in the social system.

*It is not the place of this manual to discuss the various meanings of the sociological term 'function'. The definition offered here is the most general. Other sociologists have used the term more specifically, such as those who relate function to basic needs.

(*xx*) *Socialisation:*   A process of inculcation whereby an individual learns the principal values and symbols of the social systems in which he operates and the expression of those values in the norms governing the roles which he and others enact.

(*xxi*) *Status:*   The respect and recognition accorded to an individual or role by others.

(*xxii*) *Totality:*   A social system exercising complete control over its inmates' value orientations and behaviour by providing for their basic needs within that system.

1 Goals

Organisations set out to attain specific ends or goals. In this, they differ from other social institutions, such as the family, the goals of which are unplanned and serve broader and less defined purposes.

Goals therefore may be defined as 'the state of affairs which a society exists to attain or promote'. But goals are not objective, finite entities: they consist solely in the perceptions of different members of the organisation, and different members or different groups of members may have very different views of the ends of their society. The governors, staff and pupils of a school may not conceive it as pursuing identical goals. Goals also vary in their kind. Perceived ones may be short term or long term, others may be proposed rather than actual or achieved.

The content of the goals of schools can be classified into three: instrumental, expressive, and organisational. But the relationship between these three types is not static: there is an inherent tendency for them to compete and displace one another, for example cultural activities (expressive goals) may tend to be squeezed out by academic pressures (instrumental goals). This dynamic applies too to the way goals are perceived or evaluated within the school or without. Staff and pupils, staff and parents, for example, can evaluate goals differently, as can other elements of the wider society. Conflicts therefore are built into the goal systems of schools.

1   External influences bearing on goals

The ends which schools serve are not chosen in abstract. They are conditioned by a complex of factors external or internal to the school society. Among the chief external factors are:

(*i*)   *The historical tradition in which the school stands.*
(*ii*) *The functions of the school for the wider society.*
(*iii*) *The influences of other organisations in its environment.*

(**i**) **Historical tradition** Among the forces which help define the goals which schools pursue, those of historical development are of profound importance. It is essential to isolate these historical forces if the nature of the goal-setting process is to be analysed. Here we classify the principal trends of development, the various traditions, which have shaped the differing ends of schools in England. Instrumental ends concern skills, expressive ones concern values, organisational ones concern the school's own organisation. Fuller definitions of these terms occur later.

(*a*) *The denominational tradition* has been crucial in shaping the system. Schools belonging to the Church of England, Roman Catholic, Quaker, Methodist and Baptist and Congregational Churches antedate the state system of education. They still flourish in the independent sector, and C of E and Roman Catholic schools hold a prominent place in state primary and secondary education. In these schools expressive stress will be high.

(*b*) *The Arnold tradition*, formulated in the nineteenth-century Public School, still exercises considerable influence. It stresses the training of character for those who will hold responsible positions in later life, the development of physical excellence, of leadership, a sense of service, of how to wield authority and obey it, of moral sensibility. The training of academic intelligence is highly prized as an end in itself, not necessarily as a means to examination success, still less as a training for a specific career. Creative or manual skills may not be given any such emphasis. In this tradition some instrumental, most expressive and all organisational features are given powerful emphasis, and staff-pupil relations are close but formal. It is mainly found in the Public School and the independent sector of education, but elements of the tradition are embedded in that of the State Grammar School, and of others.

1 External influences bearing on goals

(i) Historical tradition

(a) Denominational tradition
Christian religion and expressive ends high.
State Schools: C. of E., R.C.
Independent Schools: C. of E., R.C., Quaker, Methodist, Baptist, etc.

(b) Arnold tradition
High stress on character formation for responsibility, and on intellectual training. Instrumental, expressive, and organisational ends high.
State Schools: elements in Grammar and other schools.
Independent Schools: Public Schools and some others.

(c)   *The Elementary School tradition* really derives from the final crystallisation of a state system of education in 1870. Its stress lies in the imparting of rudimentary educational skills—reading, writing, manual training and vocational preparation. It is accompanied often by distant staff-pupil relations, poor buildings, culture conflict between the staff and pupils, and problems of control. Some state Primary and Secondary Modern Schools inherit this tradition. In this tradition instrumental and organisational ends are dominant in practice.

(d)   *The Grammar School tradition* derives in part from an ancient stream and in part from the Arnold tradition. Again academic intelligence is highly prized but tends to be focused more on examination performance, and there might be more vocational concern. Creative and manual expression are given low stress. Some attention is paid to the Arnoldian character training (authority —service, etc.) but this is variable. Most Independent, Direct Grant and state Grammar schools exhibit these features, and elements have percolated some of the Comprehensive and Secondary Modern Schools. The tradition is marked by high instrumental (academic only) stress, some expressive stress (which can be intense in certain schools) and considerable organisational emphasis. Staff-pupil relations are distant and formal.

(e)   *The Progressive School tradition*, though at least as old as Rousseau, practically derives from the years after the first world war. Its aim is the development of individual personality by keeping pressures on the child low; there is great freedom, low stress on purely academic or physical subjects, more stress on creative skills and manual skills, emphasis on meeting the abilities of individual children, and allowing them choice of activity and participation in decisions. Staff-pupil relations are expected to be close and informal, and psychological knowledge is utilised. Expressive goals are dominant (different ones from those in the Public School) and some instrumental ones, but organisational goals are low. The tradition is found in all self-styled Progressive Schools, in some other Independent Schools, in many State Primary and some Secondary Schools and many Special Schools.

There are many other school traditions which might have been categorised—the charity school one, the technical tradition, the evening class tradition, and so on. But the above five are the main ones.

(c) *Elementary School tradition*
Stress on rudimentary instrumental and expressive features.
Instrumental and organisational ends paramount.
State Schools: some Primary, Secondary Modern and Comprehensive Schools.
Independent Schools: little found.

(d) *Grammar tradition*
High stress on intellectual training with examination emphasis, may be considerable expressive stress in modified Arnold tradition. High instrumental stress (academic), variable expressive and high organisational emphasis.
State Schools: Grammar Schools and some others.
Independent: some Independent Schools and most Direct Grant ones.

(e) *Progressive tradition*
Stress on freedom, creative expression, education related to ability, psychological approach, participation in decisions.
State Schools: many Primary and many Secondary Modern and Comprehensive Schools have elements of this approach.
Independent Schools: 'Progressive' schools and some others.

Schools can possess aspects of several traditions. Some Public Schools are denominational and a few also have some ' progressive ' elements. Secondary Modern Schools may have parts of the Elementary, Grammar and Progressive streams in their values.

(ii) Functions for the wider society which influence goals Schools exercise three kinds of functions for the wider society: allocative ones, integrative ones and administrative ones. These functions inevitably powerfully condition goals and the school's ability to modify them.

(*a*) *Allocative functions.* Schools are one of society's principal agencies for maintaining social stratification or of ensuring mobility upwards or downwards. It is the school's role in promoting upward social mobility which has attracted so much sociological attention in Britain since the second world war. The historical forces mentioned above, the existence of separate independent and maintained sectors of education and of the tripartite division within the maintained sector, the tendency of different social groups to live in separate districts, all enhance the role of the school as a system of maintaining social stratification but limit its role in promoting upward or downward social mobility. The goals of schools, though all influenced by the social background and values of teachers, will thus be conditioned by the social stratum or strata it serves. Thus the real goals of Secondary Modern Schools, which serve by and large the children of semi-skilled or unskilled working parents, differ sharply from those of Public Schools which serve the children of upper-class parents. The educational and career expectations of these differing social groups, their varying cultural patterns, inevitably influence the schools' goals, whether the staff accept or attempt to resist the influences of the pupils' background.

(*b*) *Integrative functions.* At the same time as they help allocate the human resources of the society in different directions, schools function as a basic means by which *all* the members of society are introduced to its history, culture, values, and accepted norms, and are prepared for the roles they will play. These integrative functions of schools have four main elements: (1) the development of skills, creative powers, of ' personality '; (2) socialisation of the pupil by the transmission of the values, culture and norms of the society; (3) the delineation for the pupil of his role as child or

(ii) Functions for the wider society which influence goals

(a) *Allocative functions*
Maintaining social stratification
Enabling social mobility

(b) *Integrative functions*
Transmitting knowledge, skills
Socialising into values, norms, culture
Delineating the role of child or adolescent
Training in adult roles

adolescent in society; (4) the training of the pupil in various adult roles which he may or will take up in later life. All schools have these four integrative functions. They again are influenced by the background of staff and pupils. As teachers in English society themselves tend to be drawn from a fairly narrow social range, and are themselves integrated by processes of further education, there is among them a broad consensus on many of the skills, values, norms and culture which schools should transmit to their pupils. Nevertheless the forces of historical tradition, of parental expectation and of the subcultures in which schools are embedded, produce major differences of emphasis in integrative goals. Not only do the skills and knowledge to be transmitted differ as between, say, Grammar and Secondary Modern Schools, or between streams inside each school, but the cultural style which each kind of school presents may be different and may or may not be attuned to that of the presenting background of the pupils. In our society, the higher the socio-economic class of the pupils, the greater the correspondence of the school's culture with that of the presenting background. Schools also can differ in their provision of roles: some schools stress the childhood role, others, such as Public Schools, are more concerned with training in adult roles.

(c) *Administrative functions.* Schools operate as agents of social and medical welfare, as places where children are kept together under control, and as an agent replacing the family for short periods of time. These functions clearly shape goals most markedly and, in extremes, produce kinds of institution serving special needs.

These are the basic kinds of functions which help shape the goals of schools. We have seen that they are, in turn, profoundly influenced by (1) patterns of social stratification in the society; (2) the background and training of teachers; and (3) the social class and presenting culture of the pupils.

(c) *Administrative functions*
Agent of social and medical welfare
Keep children together under control: custodial agents
Agent replacing family for short periods of time

These functions and therefore the goals are powerfully affected by
(a) *The presenting culture of the pupils, particularly*
Social class background
Culture, values and norms of background
(b) *Presenting culture of teachers*
Social class background
Culture, values, and norms of background
Culture, values and norms of training

(iii) Organisations which influence goals The third external force which conditions the goals of schools comes from other organisations with which they come into contact in their operation.

These are, first, organisations which mediate between the school and others more marginal to it. These consist of the governors, the LEA and its officials, the inspectorate, parental organisations, former pupils' organisations, and feeding or dependent schools. All these may influence goals or the way they are set or changed.

Beyond them are other bodies: Parliament, the government and central Departments of State, universities and examination boards, employers and the youth employment service. Later on in this analysis (p. 204) these bodies are considered in the light of their functions for the operation of the school. Clearly however they, too, may affect goals in various ways fundamental or not.

These then are the factors which influence from the outside the goals which schools pursue. The rest of the analysis explains how internal forces affect the setting and achievement of those goals.

(iii) The organisational environment of the school which influences goals

    (*a*) *Mediating organisations*
        Governors
        LEA
        Inspectorate
        Parental organisations
        Old Boy organisations
        Feeding or dependent schools

    (*b*) *External organisations*
        Parliament, central department
        Universities
        Examining boards
        Employers

2 The content of goals

For the analysis of the school it is useful to distinguish between three kinds of goal: instrumental, expressive and organisational.

(*i*) *Instrumental goals* in schools are concerned with the transmission of useful skills and information or the acquisition of qualifications: such things as logical training, social poise, competence as a citizen, training for a job, physical soundness and dexterity, as well as the gaining of knowledge or of examination results. All these goals are, in one sense, the provision of skills or tools for further ends. A precise definition of *instrumental* is therefore:

> *Instrumental*: That which is a means to a further end, that which appertains to performance in the sense of necessary technical operations rather than the satisfaction induced by performance or by attainment of the end of the performance.

(*ii*) *Expressive goals* in schools are concerned with things which are not means but ultimates. Schools may set out to transmit norms or values, such as religious faith, moral codes, cultural appreciation, community or team spirit, or they may aim to foster the development of personality for its own sake or creative expression. These are not skills but ends in themselves. A precise definition of *expressive* is therefore:

> *Expressive*: That which is an end in itself (although it may have instrumental functions), that which satisfies the need disposition* of the performer as distinct from the performance, the technical operations or processes necessary to attain such satisfaction.

(*iii*) *Organisational goals* concern not the skills or values which the society sets out to develop but the machinery by which the society operates. They involve such things as ensuring that the organisation has adequate personnel, that its continuity is certain, that its reputation is unsullied, that it operates in a smooth, orderly and efficient way, and that its members are kept busy in ways which serve its other goals, or at least do not threaten its efficient running. A precise definition of *organisational* is therefore:

> *Organisational*: That which maintains an ongoing system.

---

*Need disposition may be defined as: A tendency to fulfil some requirement of the organism, a tendency to accomplish some end state, a disposition to do something with an object designed to accomplish this end state.

2 The content of goals

(i) *Instrumental*
    (a) Academic, acquisition of knowledge, mental skills
    (b) Vocational, preparation for job
    (c) Personal and social training, manners, poise
    (d) Training in being a competent citizen
    (e) Physical development and dexterity

(ii) *Expressive*
    (a) Religious, pastoral care
    (b) Ethical
    (c) Cultural
    (d) Personal development, creative expression
    (e) Sportsmanship

(iii) *Organisational*
    (a) Continuity over time: self perpetuation, recruitment, economy
    (b) Servicing the organisation (bureaucratic)
    (c) Control, order, discipline
    (d) Ensuring activity, filling in time, preventing disruption
    (e) Maintaining its reputation outside

In some senses, organisational goals fall into the category of expressive ones. As we found in fieldwork in schools, things such as order, reputation or economy sometimes became ends in themselves, and were pursued with the same devotion as expressive ends such as religion or self-expression. In most cases, it is true, they were obviously secondary to the main instrumental or expressive aims of schools. But in a few cases the school's own maintenance and machinery seemed to supersede in importance the other two. Organisational goals can thus possess their own autonomy. Though ends in themselves, they are different from pure expressive ones in that the latter concern states which may be considered of absolute value outside as well as within the society (such as faith, goodness, fulfilment of potentiality), whilst organisational ones are relative solely to the requirements of the organisation's own machinery and functioning. It is for this reason that we have separated them into a distinct category.

On page 57 we group together the main activities or features of school society under the kind of goals to which they are *chiefly* related. Of course, an activity listed under one goal may have subsidiary functions for another one. Academic work may be instrumental in the sense of acquiring mental skills, but may also be expressive, in the sense of, for example, enjoying the beauty of language. Similarly, while sport or P.E. are mainly instrumental in the way they develop physical fitness and skill, they can be expressive in the way they develop team spirit or even moral sensibility and can often be organisational too as a means of keeping energetic children occupied, or of arousing commitment to the machinery of the school, house, or form, and so on.

3 Types of goals

Just as the goals of schools vary in their structure, so too they vary in the degree to which they are pursued or perceived by the members of the society. There may be a difference between the stated goals and those really pursued, as well as between those perceived and achieved. Such differences are vital to the internal operation, the pressures within and the change of schools over time, and to comparisons between them.

We lay out these distinctions below:

(*i*) *Stated goals:*   The state of affairs which the society exists to attain or promote.

(*ii*) *Real goals:*   The state of affairs to which the resources and activities of the society are immediately directed. (This can be a long-term goal, or a means to it, or a goal which is distinct from long-term goals.)

(*iii*) *Achieved goals:*   The state of affairs the society actually attains or promotes.

(*iv*) *Proposed goals:*   The state of affairs which various groups within a society evaluate as that which the society should strive to achieve.

(*v*) *Perceived goals:*   Stated, real or achieved goals as evaluated by various groups within the society.

Goals then are neither static nor finite—in our sociological framework they are dynamic variables subject to pressures from inside and outside the school. When examining goals it is essential to bear in mind what types of goal and whose perception of them we are dealing with, and the inherent relationships between them.

3 Types of goals

(i) Stated Goals
(ii) Real Goals
(iii) Achieved Goals
(iv) Proposed Goals

All these are (v), the differently *perceived goals* of various groups within and without the society, including the researcher and his objective indices.

Stated goals may be very different from the real ones, and the perception of both by different groups of people may also differ. The proposed goals of the pupils or parents may challenge or tend to displace those stated by the governors, and the real goals of the staff may not coincide with those stated on their behalf by the head. Goals which are achieved may not always coincide with those which are stated or proposed or even perceived by some groups. Thus in a ' progressive ' school the stated, real and proposed aims of its members may set out to promote freedom and individualism but facets of its operation, such as the powerful subculture of the pupils, may produce an all-pervasive control and generally conformist behaviour.

4 Conflicts between goals and their effects

The goals of the school do not exist in an equilibrium but in a dynamic tension. This tension can produce a displacement, one or more goals gaining dominance or losing equality, and cause dysfunctions for the society. (By ' dysfunction ' we mean consequences which impair the maintenance of or prevent some trend in a social system.) Such dysfunctions may be useful for the society as they promote change or unintended attainments, but severe dysfunction can cause nonattainment of the basic goals a society strives to attain.

Here, less abstractly, are the most common goal-conflict situations found in school society. As the goals are embodied in parts of the organisation, this analysis applies to the conflicts within and between the subunits of the school as well.

  (i) The first situation is a balance between instrumental, expressive and organisational goals and their dependent subsystems.

 (ii) In the second situation the organisational goals of the school are subordinated to its other functions, as perhaps in a small Primary or Secondary School where an inspiring head or teacher enables the instrumental and expressive goals to be largely attained, though the society's organisational requirements are subordinated and may be neglected. The same can be true of larger schools pursuing ' liberal ' approaches to discipline, relationships and so on.

4 Conflicts between goals and their effects

PATTERNS OF CONFLICT

(i)   Instrumental = Expressive = Organisational

(ii) Instrumental = Expressive
        | |
            Organisational

(iii) The other situations are all dysfunctional, though not necessarily disruptive. Perhaps the most common situation is that where the school's instrumental and organisational ends dominate its expressive ones, the pattern in many day schools or colleges and some universities. Expressive ends are displaced.

(iv) Equally dysfunctional, though rare, is that where the expressive ends or structure dominate the other two and the basic instrumental and organisational ends are displaced. This can be the case in a Progressive School.

(v) Most dysfunctional, in the sense that the school is prevented from attaining its basic goals, is the case where organisational ends displace the other two. This is not just a theoretical possibility. We have found in our research some extreme cases where organisational goals such as preoccupation with order or discipline, or considerations of economy or recruitment or the domination of an organisational subsystem (the bursarial or secretarial one) notably prevented schools attaining their instrumental ends to some degree and, completely their expressive ones. In these cases the real goals varied markedly from the stated ones, and the proposed goals of the pupils were very different from those which the researchers indices showed the school was achieving.

5 Summary of goal conflicts and their effects on school society

Opposite, we lay out these models of conflicts more concisely according to the degree which they are functional, moderately dysfunctional or severely so for the achievement of goals. However what is functional for goal achievement may be dysfunctional for change (see Change, p. 166).

These patterns are basic to our subsequent discussion, for they apply both to the conflict situations between the subsystems in the school and within each subsystem itself. They enable fundamental comparisons to be made between the various sectors of the school society, between various moments of the school over time and between schools and types of schools.

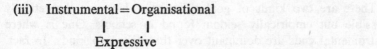

(iii)   Instrumental = Organisational

Expressive

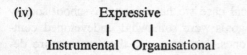

(iv)   Expressive

Instrumental   Organisational

(v)   Organisational

Instrumental   Expressive

5 Summary of goal conflicts and their effects on school society
(applicable to goals and to the subsystems for attaining them)

For the achievement
of goals

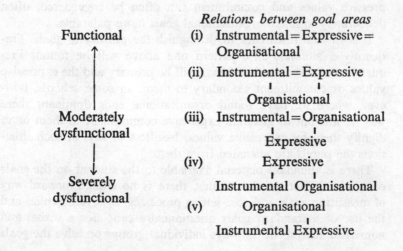

	Relations between goal areas
Functional	(i) Instrumental = Expressive = Organisational
	(ii) Instrumental = Expressive Organisational
Moderately dysfunctional	(iii) Instrumental = Organisational Expressive
	(iv) Expressive Instrumental Organisational
Severely dysfunctional	(v) Organisational Instrumental Expressive

There are two kinds of goal situations which are theoretically possible but empirically seldom found in schools. One is where instrumental ends are dominant over the other two kinds. In fact, instrumental ends always demand an elaborate and efficient organisational structure for their fulfilment, so the two goals usually go together. In one exceptional case we have found a school society where the organisational goals were somewhat undeveloped compared with instrumental ones, but even so, they were more developed than the expressive ones. Such a rare case is dysfunctional.

The second empirical improbability is the dominance of expressive and organisational ends over instrumental ones. In fact expressive and organisational goals can be incompatible and may conflict: the demands of organisational efficiency and maintenance of order, discipline, reputation, routine, and so on, do not coincide with the goals of transmitting some kinds of values, of development of personality, of self-expression and so on. Thus a school's pastoral goals often conflict with its disciplinary ones, its aim of developing critical faculties may conflict with compulsory routines, and its goal of individual self expression may conflict with that of outside reputation. Such conflicts are sharpened, as we shall see, by the incompatible structures and methods often used to attain these two kinds of goals. This combination of ends is thus not found in practice. What *is* found in practice is the generation of expressive commitment to organisational ends or practices. Around such things as school reputation, or organisational devices such as houses, expressive values and commitment can often be engendered, often deliberately to make organisational goals more palatable.

It is for the researcher to distinguish the priority in goals. Frequently a situation like pattern one above will be found. Frequently, too, organisational ends will be primary and the expressive values or commitment secondary to them. In some schools, however, where we have found organisational ends dominant there was no attempt to generate expressive commitment to them or to dignify them by expressive values. Needless to say, in such situations the pupils are alienated from them.

There is abundant material available to the student on the goals of a school. But despite all this, there is no straightforward way of measuring goals and goal-setting processes. Interview replies and the use of a standard goals questionnaire can offer a verbal and numerical analysis of the ways individual groups perceive the goals

Seldom found   (vi)   Instrumental

Expressive   Organisational

(vii)   Expressive = Organisational

Instrumental

of the school and an assessment of the effectiveness of the organisation. Numerical scores which result from these tests illustrate the perceptions and consensus of a large number of people but oversimplify the situation and remove the possibility of any qualifications or subtleties. Interview material on the other hand is not readily reduced to scores or indices, even though it offers the individual an opportunity to discuss problems in full.

Stated and real goals can be derived from speeches, documents, notices and minutes, while replies to interviews given in the methodology below (p. 245) (headmaster's interview qq. 17, 18; housemaster's interview qq. 15, 16) provide further material and evidence on proposed and achieved goals (headmaster q. 6; housemaster q. 11). We have devised a goals questionnaire (q. 1) which enables the perception of the various kinds of goals on the part of staff, parents and pupils to be assessed and expressed in quantitative fashion by scores. Further questions (70, 72, 74, 75, 76, 77, 78, 79, 80, 81, 90) on change, discontent, attitudes and adaptation provide other data on the perception and achievement of goals. The scale which we have devised, to measure control in a school (see chapter III) is also a valuable objective index of real goals and a check on stated ones.

Nevertheless, none of this material gives a straightforward measure of the outcome of the goal conflicts. This can only be assessed by examining the degree to which one set of evidence supports another set of evidence. For example, the stated goals of free self expression stated by the staff may not be supported by evidence of real goals inferred from a high level of institutional control or by other results indicating pupil frustration. Evidence can only be compared if a general classificatory framework is devised and each set of evidence is then interrelated.

We have examined the forces influencing goals, analysed the ways goals differ and the way different groups in the society evaluate and pursue them. The inherent conflicts between various goals have also been discussed. Now we examine the ways in which the organisation seeks to attain these goals and we look first at the subsystems which make up the school society. This is followed by a discussion of the ways pupils are fitted into the school, oriented to these goals and controlled.

6 Bibliography

The following texts are relevant to the analysis of goals:

B. B. Berk 1966; B. R. Clark 1956; H. O. Dahlke 1958; A. Etzioni 1962; B. J. Georgopolous 1959; O. Grusky 1959; H. Jones 1965; T. W. G. Miller 1961; P. Nokes 1960; T. Parsons 1951; R. L. Simpson 1962; F. M. Stevens 1960; J. D. Thompson 1958.

II Subunits

1 Types of subunit

To attain the goals which we have outlined the school is formally structured into numerous subunits and those we have found most significant, such as the academic subunit, are listed opposite. As subunits are miniature societies in their own right they could be studied as systems in themselves, but, because our concern is their functions for the organisation, we relate them to the goals the subunits serve. As they inevitably share the conflicts which we have seen inherent in the pursuit of differing groups of goals, we look at the autonomy of individual subunits, the communication between them and outline the principal conflict situations.

2 Subunits related to goals of school

Here we take the principal subunits and relate them to the goals which they exist to promote. Thus the academic unit serves obvious instrumental and expressive goals but also indirect organisational ones, while the athletic unit serves instrumental ones (physical development) but may, according to the school, serve to differing degrees expressive ends (team spirit, leadership) and organisational ones (filling in time, keeping order). Likewise religion in schools serves obvious expressive ends (faith and development of values) and instrumental ones (imparting of knowledge, textual skills, pastoral care) but, in differing degrees may also serve some important organisation areas (promoting group consciousness, acting as a means of control or even administration). Individual departments can be assessed in this way. The degree to which the subunits serve differing goals is a major differentiating factor between schools. For example in some schools, day or residential, the house is a purely administrative unit which may or may not serve some instrumental ends such as training pupils in control, but in others it serves fundamental and dominant expressive ends such as the instilling of values or commitment. All the subunits listed above can be so classified and the differences between schools will be significant.

1 Types of subunit

(i) Academic Departments including library
(ii) Athletic
(iii) Religious
(iv) Main units of social interaction (e.g. house, form)
(v) Pastoral unit separate from house (e.g. tutor/counselling systems)
(vi) Societies
(vii) Domestic, catering
(viii) Bursarial and secretarial
(ix) Medical (matrons, nurse, doctor, etc.)
(x) Ex-pupils association
(xi) Parents Association
(xii) Governing Body

2 Subunits related to goals of school

(The brackets indicate that there will be variations across the schools in the extent to which the particular subunit will serve such goals.)

Instrumental	Expressive	Organisational
Academic	Academic	(Academic)
Athletic	(Athletic)	(Athletic)
(Religious)	Religious	(Religious)
(House)	(House)	House
—	Pastoral	(Pastoral)
Societies	Societies	(Societies)
—	—	Bursarial + Secretarial
—	—	Medical
—	(Old Pupils)	Old Pupils
—	(Parents organisation)	Parents organisation
—	(Governors)	Governors

Such a classification can valuably be done within subunits e.g. for the library, the science department, etc.

3   The autonomy of subunits and the federal or centralised structure of the school

Subunits differ in the degree to which they are autonomous within the schools society, and, according to the number of autonomous subunits, schools differ in the degree to which they are federal or centralised structures. This is a basic difference between schools and between the units within each school.

The dimensions opposite enable a subunit to be measured for its autonomy. The more a subunit possesses the features *downwards* on the dimension the more it is autonomous. Obviously the greater the number of autonomous units a school possesses the more federal it is.

Thus the house unit, the science department or other departments, the religious unit, the bursarial and medical units, or even the library, can all be more or less autonomous with their own goals and separate roles but may or may not possess their own internal hierarchies, separate personnel or buildings.

3 The autonomy of subunits and the federal or centralised structure of the school

Centralised school structure, subunits coincident with general structure

|

Increasing
Autonomy

|

Degree of autonomy *increases* the more the subunit has features which come at the *lower* end of the list

|

↓

Subunits autonomous: Federal school structure

Subunits

Separate role system or offices (all subunits will possess this by definition)

Separate hierarchy of status

Separate formal communication system

Separate authority system

Separate culture (norms, traditions and rituals)

Separate territories delineated (but shared in time and use with other subunits)

Separate line (assistant) personnel

Separate staff (professional) personnel

Separate physical plant, building

Separate decision-making mechanism

4   Conflict situations between subunits

Subunits generate conflict situations, a dynamic disequilibrium which follows that of the goals they serve. For example there is often conflict between the athletic subunit and the medical subunit when crucial athletes are classed as unfit. If the reader looks back to the section where goal conflict was described (p. 65) he can see how the subunits will tend to conflict and which are likely to prove dysfunctional for the society. Here we simply lay out the principal conflict situations.

Two major subunits, the academic and the main units of social interaction, are now discussed in greater detail.

A significant factor influencing the extent and degree of conflict between subunits and closely related to the process of decision-making is the method of communication that exists between the subunits, and the classification we have found useful follows at the end of the chapter.

5   Example 1: the academic subunit

The first example of a subunit, the academic, is one of the easiest to approach. In all schools there is a wealth of material on curriculum, academic performance, subject choices, etc. and with definite hypotheses in mind it is possible to elicit and enter up the necessary information. Opposite are some examples of what we have found useful, but they obviously make no attempt to exhaust the mass of empirical data available. Other subunits such as the Governing Body would present much greater difficulties in analysis. This simple approach to the academic unit is followed by a discussion of more complex and equally critical subunits, that of the basic units of social interaction such as the form.

4 Conflict situations between subunits

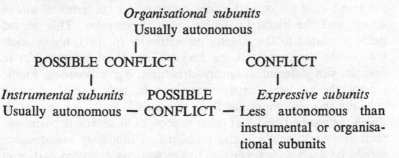

Within each subunit there will be conflict between organisational functions and expressive ones, and perhaps between expressive functions and instrumental ones. Conflict between organisational and instrumental functions is less likely (see p. 66).

5 Example 1: The academic subunit

(i) Number and hierarchy of departments Details are given of
the number of major and minor departments (in terms of allow-
ances) and the hierarchy within each department. This second
point is related to the chapter on authority (p. 181), for in some
schools the department is the major hierarchical subunit. Yet in
schools with different authority structures, e.g. a boarding Public
School, the academic departments may be only several of many
subunits and less important than others such as the house unit. It
should be remembered that other aspects of academic departments
such as power, conflicts and problems of boundary maintenance
should be dealt with according to the sections discussed earlier in
this chapter and later in the book (pp. 183 and 205).

In order to assess differences in the academic structures of
schools, the degree of autonomy of each of its components should
be assessed in the way previously suggested (p. 75). It is then possible to relate the academic departments to other aspects of school
structure, to analyse the balance between different departments
within the academic system of the school and make comparisons
between schools.

(ii) Details of the academic departments This covers the curriculum arrangements, the subjects taught, numbers in groups, leaving
rate, and the fate of leavers.

Most of this data is acquired from form lists and interview with
the second master (usually he is in charge of academic administration, time-tables for example). The summaries are not a substitute
for notes on the details of courses.

Objective indices for such things as fifth form drop-out rates in
schools with sixth forms can easily be devised if comparison
between schools is required.

(i) Number and hierarchy of departments
   (a) *Number of departments*:
      List major academic departments
      List minor academic departments
      List other posts of special responsibility receiving an allowance
   (b) *Hierarchy of departments*:
      Number of graded posts in major academic departments
      Number of non-teaching positions in major academic departments

(ii) Details of the academic departments
   (a) *Subjects taught in school*:
      Arts:
      Science:
      Other:
   (b) *Number in school taking exams this year and results in previous years*
      CSE:
      'O' level:
      'A' level:
      University scholarship:
      Other specify:
   (c) *Average size of teaching unit for main subjects*
      on entry
      after two years in school
      O level
      post O level

The numbers leaving and careers taken up are found from the annual return the school makes to the Department of Education and Science and from the careers master.

The numbers expelled or ('asked to leave prematurely for disciplinary reasons') is easily found from the pupils. Staff assessment of this figure may not be accurate.

These later sections deal with the setting, streaming and teaching.

The criteria for streaming and setting: the point at which it begins and the type of subjects involved are analysed.

This last analysis concerns the way teaching groups move up the school. The categories by year, term and ability are not exclusive.

These last sections examine the types of teaching found in the school.

The approach to teaching includes latest teaching aids, programmes, new syllabuses such as the new maths and subjects such as social sciences, Russian, etc.

This section on the academic subunit has dealt with details easily found from documents, interviews with staff and pupils. The more intangible things, which many would consider more relevant, like the quality of staff-pupil relations and responses of the pupils are discussed later in chapter IV. All this empirical material is useful but it is important to bear in mind the more abstract dimensions by which subunits can be compared—goals served, autonomy, conflict, which were discussed earlier in the chapter. Much information on these general matters will come to light when gathering the empirical details.

In this Manual, we treat the academic subsystem rather empirically. This is because our concepts revolve round the idea of goals and structures. An interesting and alternative approach starts with the basic academic subsystem and examines the way combinations of subjects and methods of teaching determine the social structure of the school. In Primary Schools, for example, the introduction of small-group flexible teaching has changed many basic relationships in the school. Valuable research using this approach is being done by Professor Basil Bernstein's Research Unit at the Institute of Education, London.

(d) *Further education and leaving* Boys Girls
Numbers in Vth last year
Number who went into VIth form
Number who left
Destination of leavers
Numbers asked to leave prematurely for disci-
plinary reasons in last academic year
(e) *Streaming/Setting*
State the criteria for streaming, setting and the
point at which streaming and setting begin
(f) *Type of setting*
for all subjects
for limited subjects
(g) *Mobility in school*
Movement up school: CLASS SET STREAM
by year
by term
by ability
(h) *Means of teaching* Pre O level Post O level
Group or classroom teaching
Tutorial supervision
Private tuition (paid)
(i) *Approach to teaching*
Films
TV
Language laboratory teaching machines
New syllabuses
Creativity labs.
New subjects
Closed circuit TV

6   Example 2: the basic units of social interaction

Most schools have some basic form of social organisation for organisational purposes, such as checking registers, or keeping control; for instrumental purposes, such as giving their pupils experience in management; or for expressive purposes such as instilling
values or exercising pastoral care over pupils. These units differ
from school to school in the degree to which they are expressively
oriented: in some schools the form or tutorial group or house
exists just for organisational purposes. In others, however, they have
expressive functions, possessing their own structure and generat-
ing their own values, norms and culture. The framework opposite
illustrates from top to bottom for each basic unit the structural
features which will be found if it is purely organisational (top) or
also expressive (bottom) in its operation.

These units also differ in the degree to which they are coincidental
with the school's general or academic organisation or are articulated from it. Our framework then proceeds from left to right in
order of increasing autonomy of the social unit from the basic
academic structure of the school.

The highest degree of autonomy and of expressive operation go
together in the tutorial or house situations delineated in the bottom
right-hand corner: this kind of house organisation could apply to
that of a large Comprehensive Day School or to most residential
schools. In some large schools still broader age groups can be
organised into subunits of considerable autonomy, as, for example,
separate upper and lower schools with a senior master in charge.

6 Example 2: The basic units of social interaction

Degree to which they serve expressive functions and are autonomous

TYPE OF UNIT

Functions served by the subunit	Form Unit	Tutor System	House System
Organisational and Instrumental	No separate staff role no separate timetable period no separate pupil hierarchy no separate permanent base	based on form unit limited to academic matters	separate staff role (housemaster) separate unit for control games } conduct } competitions work } no separate timetable period no separate building no separate pupil hierarchy (e.g. house prefects)
Expressive and Organisational and Instrumental	separate staff role separate timetable period separate pupil hierarchy separate and permanent base	separate staff role separate from form separate timetable periods separate base (e.g. tutor room) separate personnel (e.g. outside counsellors)	separate staff role separate unit for control (games, conduct, work) separate timetable periods separate territory or buildings separate pupil hierarchy (house prefects or officers) separate professional personnel (housemaster paid as such) separate domestic personnel (housemen, domestics, etc.)

Subunits integrated in the school's academic subsystem ←————————→ Subunits autonomous and independent of the school's academic subsystem.

7 Difference in reputation for main units of social interaction

Social units differ in their perceived characteristics.

A list of opposites covering variations frequently found in schools is given to staff and pupils after an open-ended question about characteristics and reputation has been given in housemaster and prefects interviews. The list should be given to as many people as possible (headmaster interview q. 12, housemaster q. 9).

Obviously there may be big differences between individual assessments, as people tend to be loyal to their houses or groups. An accurate assessment for *all* groups will be impossible to achieve. Nevertheless, what clearly emerges is which of the groups stands out in certain categories. Pupils will soon point out the forms or groups that are strict, have no 'spirit', or have trouble makers. Most groups will be neutral when all assessments are rated but a few will be prominent on certain criteria.

8 Communications among the subunits

How do these subunits and offices communicate with one another? We consider the formal methods of communication, which may be defined as 'formal association for the purpose of discussion or making decisions'. The communication system links and relates all the subunits in the formal society. It is closely related to the process of decision-making.

An important distinction must be made between *horizontal* and *vertical* communications.

Horizontal Communication: Communication among individuals of similar position in the authority hierarchy of the organisation.

Vertical Communication: Communication among individuals of different positions in the hierarchy of the organisation.

Each of these types of communication (horizontal and vertical) is then analysed according to:

(a) *The complexity of the communication process* (i.e. the number of positions involved, whether few or many);

(b) *the degree of formalisation* (whether or not the meeting have agendas, minutes or records, or are conducted formally);

(c) the *frequency* of meetings (regularly or just once per term) and this gives us the following types of communication:

7 Difference in reputation for main units of social interaction

Lax	Rigid
Scruffy	Smart
Dull	Clever
Unintellectual	Intellectual
Unfriendly	Friendly
Unsportive	Sportive
Uncreative	Creative
Bad behaviour	Good behaviour
'Square'	'Trendy'
No initiative	Initiative
Not homely	Homely
Dirty	Clean

(Repeat for each social unit)

8 Communications among the subunits

(i) For horizontal communication

(a) *Complex, formal and frequent*: Provision for horizontal communication at many levels, e.g. housemasters, heads of departments, staff, heads of house, prefects, sixth form, meetings of each year or its representatives.

(b) *Complex, formal and infrequent*: Same as above but more infrequently used.

(c) *Limited, formal, frequent*: Provision for horizontal communication at a few levels only, e.g. staff meetings, prefect meetings.

(d) *Limited, formal, infrequent*: Same as above but infrequent.

(ii) Similarly, for vertical communication

(a) *Complex, formalised and frequent*: Regular committees of senior staff and junior staff and pupils—food committee, social committee, housemasters or senior staff and prefects, etc.

(b) *Formal and simple*: Regular but only in a few areas, e.g. housemaster and prefect meetings, headmaster and prefect meetings only.

(c) *Complex and informal*: Informal and regular meetings between most groups.

(d) *Simple and informal*: Informal meetings between just a few groups, e.g. headmaster and prefects only.

These are summarised on the opposite page.

Most information is found in interviews with the staff, with the headmaster qq. 3, 10, and pupils, particularly head boy and heads of houses. The perception of decision-making test and observations of notices and minutes, files and so on provide further data.

(i) Horizontal communication
  (a) Complex and formalised; frequently used
  (b) Complex and formalised; infrequently used
  (c) Limited and formalised; frequent
  (d) Limited and formalised; infrequent

(ii) Vertical communication
  (a) Complex, formalised and frequent
  (b) Simple and formalised
  (c) Complex and informal
  (d) Simple and informal

9 Types of communication in goal areas

We can now relate these processes of communication to the goal areas defined in the last chapter. This enables us to see that while horizontal communication alone may be functional for instrumental areas, for expressive areas there must be considerable vertical communication to involve the pupils with expressive ends. For organisational areas, horizontal communication alone may be functional, but, where organisational goals tend to dominate over expressive and instrumental ones, considerable alienation will occur amongst the pupils unless a more vertical communication system is adopted. A good illustration of this is the abolition of fagging in a Public School, which can result in a breakdown in vertical communication and lead to unexpected alienation amongst the junior pupils whom the measure was intended to benefit. They receive orders but take no part in the framing of them, they are not involved in any vertical communications.

10 Bibliography

The following texts are relevant to the chapter on subunits:
The Academic subunit:
J. S. Coleman 1961; R. R. Dale 1962, 1963, 1964, 1965; J. C. Daniels 1961; N. L. Gage 1963; J. W. Halliwell 1964; B. Jackson 1964; W. F. Koontz 1962; C. Lacey 1966; R. Lynn 1959; C. D. Orth 1962; T. Parsons 1961; A. Passow 1966; W. Pattinson 1963; D. A. Pidgeon 1959; W. G. A. Rudd 1958, 1960; P. Street 1962; M. B. Sutherland 1961; N. Svenson 1963; E. P. Torrance 1962; C. J. Willig 1963; N. H. Wilson 1960; A. Yates 1960.

Social units:
M. C. Albrow 1966; K. Brill 1964; B. Bettelheim 1950; M. Burn 1956; J. C. Dancy 1963; A. Giddens 1960; W. Taylor 1965.

Communications:
S. Kosefsky 1958; R. L. Simpson 1959.

We turn now from the social structure of the school, that is the subunits and their interrelationships, to look at the ways pupils are assimilated into the school and the methods the school employs to motivate the children to approved goals.

9 Types of communication in goal areas

	Type	*Instrumental*	*Expressive*	*Organisational*
Horizontal	1			
Communication	2			
	3			
	4			
Vertical	1			
Communication	2			
	3			
	4			

(The types are those previously laid out in the section on mechanisms of communication.)

III Control

The attainment of goals depends partly on the successful socialisation and orientation of pupils and staff to the norms of the formal social order. Once they have been initially socialised the formal order employs other controls to reduce or prevent any deviance.* The processes of control are, therefore, 'mechanisms for maintenance of consensus on value orientations or by which motivation is kept at a level and in the direction necessary for the continuing of the operation of the social system towards its ends'.

These controls can be classified into five categories and each type is dealt with in separate sections of this chapter.

Every person who holds an official position in the formal order is guided by certain conditions of appointment and tenure which limit his or her activities. These conditions are an example of the first category of social control called structural control over office. In addition to these controls everyone in the school, including the office holders are subject to sanctions or rewards resulting from their conformist or deviant actions. The manner in which the school is structured can also exercise control over the lives of the pupils for the institutional structure controls activities, free time, social relations and opportunities for personal expression. A scale is given in the methodology which attempts to quantify the level of this kind of control in various areas. Obviously our scale was constructed for boarding schools but a similar technique can be developed for day school situations.

In addition to all these controls however there are other processes in the school which socialise and orient pupils and staff to the goals and norms of the formal social order. These processes are important because many goals, such as academic and cultural ones, take a long time to attain and thus constant orientation is required if they are to be achieved. Among these processes of orientation are assimilative and expressive controls. A scale for the quantification of the level of expressive control is given in the methodology. At the same time as these controls are wielded by the formal social order, pupils and staff are socialised and controlled

* Deviance may be defined as 'failure to conform to institutionalised norms'.

by another social order: *the informal social order*. This can be defined as 'norms, values and relationships not ordained by the goal structure but which may have functions for it'. Pupils control one another by having their own codes of behaviour and fashion. These may or may not reinforce the controls of the formal order. Where the norms of the formal and informal orders are antagonistic a pupil who is rewarded in the formal order by gaining staff approval may be sanctioned by the pupils' informal order which labels him as 'a creep'. The processes of socialisation and control by the informal social order are dealt with in section 5.

1 Structural controls over office

This section examines one device used for purposes of control. It concerns the institutionalised procedures for appointing and dismissing officers, the systems of promotion, selection and dismissal. Each major staff and pupil position in the school is controlled in this way and the process ensures that only those individuals acceptable to the formal order take on or maintain positions of formal status or authority. Some of these controls are extremely obvious but their importance should not be underestimated.

2 Control by rewards and sanctions

We have examined the ways in which staff and pupils are controlled in the process of appointment to formal positions of responsibility. Now we examine the actual rewards and sanctions all staff and pupils receive for conformity or deviance.

Three types of sanction and reward are examined: coercive, utilitarian and normative.

Coercive: Implies the use of force or coercion and covers sanctions such as caning or expulsion. Obviously there are no coercive rewards.

Utilitarian: Is concerned with the award or removal of some facility or amenity of no status value or significance for others. Fines for lost property are an example of this kind of control.

Normative: Is concerned with the award or removal of status which is of significance to others such as the demotion of a prefect or other status holder.

Many controls fall into two of these categories. A punishment such as making a pupil eat alone can be coercive, utilitarian or normative depending on the context.

Obviously all controls have some normative functions, for the aim is to orient people to goals, but the actual sanctions and rewards employed need not be normative. We have found that it is not the kinds of control employed in themselves but the way the control is evaluated in the informal orders of pupils and staff that determines the response.

1 Structural controls over office

Examine the degree to which key staff and pupil positions are controlled by:
    Selection
    Observation before appointment
    Trial, probationary periods
    Possibility of loss of office, removal from position

2 Control by rewards and sanctions

SANCTIONS:

Coercive: Beating, cane, physical force, runs, changing dress
             Expulsion

Utilitarian: Removal of amenity, e.g. privacy
                Dietary punishment
                Fine

Normative: Deprivation of status or authority position
              Promotion withheld
              Loss of privileges
              Public censure or telling off
              Private censure or telling off
              Degradation, fatigues
              Reports: internal, external
              Contact with parents by talks or letters

REWARDS:

Coercive:	By definition cannot exist
Utilitarian:	Material rewards, food, money Privacy
Normative:	Awards of privileges and status Promotion to a specific position Use of insignia (ties, badges, etc.) Competition, award for the best in the school Group approval Individual approval School's reputation Accommodation, privacy

Sanctions and rewards: distribution among officers and pupils

Next it is necessary to discuss those who wield and receive sanctions and rewards. The chart opposite shows which officers hold most responsibility for control and examines the methods which they are permitted to employ in order to perform the roles required by nature of their position.

Rewards and sanctions are also examined from the pupils' point of view and the types of sanctions and rewards pupils of different ages are likely to receive are given. In most schools there will be a move away from coercive sanctions as pupils get older. What is more, the type of sanction and reward received may differ for conformity and deviance in instrumental, expressive and organisational areas so that a coercive sanction may be applied to a pupil who misses class while a normative sanction may be applied for missing a games practice.

Some methods of control may be dysfunctional for goal achievement if they are applied to certain areas. Coercive sanctions are probably dysfunctional if they are applied to counteract deviance in expressive areas, such as beating a boy who refuses to pray in assembly.

As control is so central to the school's daily working we now extend the brief of this part of the manual and offer an example of the ways testable hypotheses can be derived from the classification of sanctions and rewards and of goals. This should demonstrate the link between theory at the conceptual, typological level and hypotheses confirmed or rejected as a result of investigation.

Sanctions and rewards: distribution among officers and pupils

	Sanctions Rewards	Sanctions and Rewards	
	Coercive	Utilitarian	Normative
Officer wielding sanctions and rewards			
Headmaster			
Senior master			
Housemaster	(i) — (iii)	(i) — (iii)	(i) — (viii)
Form master			
etc.			
Head of school			
Prefects		(i) — (ii)	(i) — (viii)
etc.			
Pupils receiving sanctions and rewards			
Prefects			
Sixth form			
Fifth, third, first form			
etc.			

Patterns of formal control towards goals   Certain modes of formal control are more functional for some of the goals pursued by schools than others. Conversely, the attainment of goals can be obstructed or prevented by the responses to the kind of control used.

In pursuing *organisational ends*, those involving order, routine and self-maintenance, and so on, all three kinds of formal control are functional. In practice, however, in day schools, utilitarian and coercive control will tend to predominate. In boarding schools, where the problems of routine, order and reputation are greater, normative control, will be more frequently used: control may not be chiefly by external regulations or inducements but by the use of norms to which the pupil society subscribes.

Instrumental ends, however, those concerning the transmission of skills, require a different pattern of formal control. Normative and utilitarian methods are more compatible with the attainment of these goals, but coercive control can obstruct the process, by the alienation caused.

Expressive ends, those concerned with the development of values or personality, are dependent on normative methods of control for their attainment. If utilitarian control is prominent, expressive ends may be devalued in the eyes of pupils. This can be the case in schools where there are material inducements for pupils to attend cultural functions. Coercive controls are severely dysfunctional for many expressive ends because the development of values cannot be externally enforced or exacted and their development can be checked by coercive methods. According to their incidence, coercive controls thus produce alienation from those ends, or, as we shall see in chapter IV retreatism or ritualism. There are many examples of this. Compulsory attendance at school cultural functions, frequent compulsory religious worship, pervasive coercive controls over areas of self expression in taste, dress, are frequently found in schools.

These analytic distinctions enable comparisons to be made between individual classroom techniques and performances, between the nature of and pupil responses to houses or tutor units, and between the nature or effectiveness of school societies as wholes.

As we saw earlier (p. 63), the goals and the subunits serving them do not form an equilibrium. Where one goal is dominant, the form of control it employs may be all pervasive in the school. In

Patterns of formal control towards goals

Goals served	*Controls employed*
Organisational	Utilitarian—Coercive*
	Normative
Instrumental	Utilitarian—Normative
	Coercive
Expressive	Normative
	Utilitarian—Coercive

Modes of control will be affected by that used for a dominant goal or subunit so that:

(a) Where organisational ends are dominant using coercive methods, coercive methods will predominate in the other areas.

(b) When expressive ends are dominant using normative methods, normative controls will predominate in the other goal areas.

* In some boarding schools the pattern appears to be: Coercive—Utilitarian—Normative

those schools in which order goals predominate with coercive methods, coercive methods will also be prominent in the instrumental and expressive sphere—hence there will be relatively low attainments of the latter. In those schools with dominant expressive aims and structures, normative control will be all pervasive, the school will function because the pupils internalise the formal norms regarding all goal areas (including organisational ones). In such schools patterns of informal social control will be congruent with the formal ones. This is the case with some Public Schools and Progressive Schools.

3 Scale of institutional control

The third method of social control is institutional control and in the methodology we offer a scale that we have used to quantify this in boarding schools.

The scale of institutional control is an attempt to devise an objective measure or standard between all schools, to assess the degree to which the school controls various aspects of the lives of the pupils by the nature of its structure and working. It not only examines the rules on freedom but takes into account restrictions on such things as activities and privacy. The numerical scores are, of course, somewhat arbitrary but the figures have been devised after lengthy discussion and testing. The scale could easily be adapted to apply to day schools.

Details of the scores are given on pp. 317–323. The scale is divided into seven areas. Comparison between schools by area is probably more significant than comparison by totals.

Many of the institutional controls do have other educational or social functions. The absence of a lavatory door may promote self-confidence or group living but it also controls private or secret activities such as smoking and so may be considered an institutional control.

3 Scale of institutional control

Give scores for each area on the scale of institutional control:
   (i) Compulsory activities
   (ii) Restrictions
   (iii) Movement, activity
   (iv) Social relations
   (v) Time
   (vi) Privacy
   (vii) Day boys in a boarding school

TOTAL: _____

4   Orientation to goal attainment

Apart from those controls that impinge directly on the individual by laying down of rules, rewards and sanctions, there are other important processes by which the school orients staff and pupils to its ends. Many of these are intangible, social psychological processes which are difficult to analyse systematically. Nevertheless, as processes of control they form an important category, especially in schools which emphasise expressive ends.

(i)   Assimilation processes   Assimilation refers to the process of ' breaking new pupils in ', or teaching them the ways and behaviour expected of them by the formal social order. It is one means of socialising pupils.

Some schools have special assimilation *units* where new pupils spend their first term or year in the school. Some of these units are distinct from the main school, others are part of the main school but physically separate with a specific member of staff in charge.

In most cases, pupils have been pre-socialised in their previous schools. The academic attitudes of teachers and pupils in top stream Junior Schools prepares for Grammar School education and this socialisation is even more manifest in Preparatory Schools from which pupils go on to Public Schools.

4 Orientation to goal attainment

(i) Assimilation processes

RULES:	(a) Periods when rules may not apply to new pupils
	(b) Special rules for new pupils
ROUTINE:	(a) Period when new pupils excused from routine
	(b) Special routine evolved for new pupils
RELATIONS WITH SENIOR PUPILS:	(a) New pupils assigned to an older pupil to assist settling in
	(b) Made a fag to an older pupil
STAFF RELATIONS:	(a) Assigned to a member or members of staff for a period
EXAMINATION:	(a) Special examination on school matters for new pupils
PRIVILEGES:	(a) New pupils accorded special privileges
	(b) Privileges withheld from new pupils
INSIGNIA:	(a) Insignia or dress to distinguish new pupils
RITUALS:	(a) Rituals associated with ending of assimilation periods
RELATIONS WITH HOME: (for residential schools only)	(a) Extra provision made for new pupils to keep contact with home
	(b) Contact from home withheld while new pupils settle in

(ii) Goal orientation This section continues the assimilation process. Assimilation deals mainly with new pupils and 'breaking them in'. Goal orientation examines the ways the attention of *all* the pupils is constantly attuned to the goals of the school.

Ten devices commonly used are defined here and the observer has to assess to what degree each device is used for each of the goal areas defined earlier. Religious sermons, and meetings are often used, for example, to foster loyalty, self discipline and even hard work and sportsmanship in some schools. Each device is common but the goals they serve can vary greatly between schools.

(ii) Goal orientation

GOALS

Instrumental Expressive Organisational

Methods:

Time: allocation of time towards stated ends
Supervision: supervision of time
Activities: control of permitted activities
Compulsory activities:
Religion:
Competition:
Rules:
Tradition:
Rituals:
Taste:

(iii) Expressive control The prosecution of expressive goals necessitates constant and intensive pupil orientation, as unlike instrumental goals, where rewards like examination results or first jobs are immediately apparent, expressive goals are intangible states, ' a Christian Gentleman ', or ' a tolerant personality '.

The scale given in the methodology tries to measure and quantify the degree to which the school attempts to orientate its pupils to expressive ends. It duplicates some of the features of the scale of institutional control which are relevant to expressive areas. But again it should be emphasised that the significance lies in the comparison between areas of school life rather than overall total scores of control. One problem is that it is less easy to devise objective indices for this scale as so many methods of orientation are intangible (e.g. arousing loyalty in chapel sermons). We have tried to use objective indices, and to avoid subjective assessments of the kind ' are sermons used to foster loyalty—a lot or a little?'. Unfortunately, certain kinds of expressive control, for example that in ' progressive' schools, are not easily reduced to such indices.

There is no necessary connection between the total scores in the two scales we have provided. Many schools which are low on one score highly on the other and vice versa.

	Typical State School	Typical Public School	Typical Progressive School
Scale of institutional control	Medium (varies greatly)	High	Low
Scale of expressive control	Low	High	High

Both these scales *together* must be taken into account when the so-called *totality* of the school is discussed. (Totality may be defined as: ' a social system exercising complete control over its inmates' value orientations and behaviour by providing for their basic needs within that system '.)

Much sociological literature has concentrated on aspects of totality measured in the scale of institutional control (for example, the work of Goffman). We maintain that to use the concept usefully for the English boarding school, both dimensions of totality must be analysed: the institutional control and the degree of expressive orientation. Evidence from the Progressive Schools demonstrates that low totality in the institutional control sphere does not automatically imply low totality in the expressive orien-

(iii) Scale of expressive control

Give scores in each area on the scale of expressive control:
Games ....
Religion ....
Leadership ....
Style of Life ....   TOTAL: ....

tation sphere for in this latter many progressive schools may be considered total.

A similar scale can be constructed for day schools.

(iv) Extracurricular activities There are many other ways in which the school orients the pupils to the ends of the school. The cultural front, buildings, uniforms, traditions, rituals and taste set by staff are all examples of the methods used.

We give one illustration of these, the extracurricular activities which are a means of orientating pupils to the goals of the school when they are *outside* the classroom by channelling their interests into approved activities.

The details can be found to some degree in the prospectus and administrative documents where a list will often be found but this is normally inaccurate. The real situation must be found out from reports and from pupils. Unofficial activities can only be found out from pupils.

Once the list of activities has been compiled, it is useful to classify these according to the goals they serve. The stated goals of the school were assessed in chapter I and it should not be difficult with these clearly established typologies to relate the two categories. The participation questions in the pupil questionnaire, qq. 6 and 7, are useful, as is the observer's attendance and participation in activities.

The internal structure and relations of activities as subunits was classified in the chapter on subunits.

Not all activities serve the official goals of the school. In some schools activities, pop clubs, wine-making and even soccer fall into this unofficial or illicit category. Pupils usually offer information about informal activities when interviewed or asked to write down lists of all activities they take part in. This is always a popular question among children.

After looking at this example, we now consider the mechanisms of social control enforced by members of a group over one another.

(iv) Extracurricular activities

(a) List all activities recognised by school and give number of pupils involved

(b) State the number of these activities which nominally serve the school's official goals

Number of pupils involved

Instrumental   Academic
Vocational
Social training
Citizenship
Physical

Expressive   Religious
Ethical
Cultural/creative
Personal development
Homeliness

Organisational   Continuity over time, self perpetuation
Servicing the organisation, bureaucratic
Control, order
Filling in time, keeping them occupied
Maintaining reputation outside

Number of official activities not serving the school's official goals:

Number of informal activities (i.e. with membership not open to everyone and not officially recognised)

Summary: Number of activities oriented towards school's stated goals:

Number not so oriented:

5 Informal control

The controls discussed so far have all examined the ways the school directs pupils to its goals and checks those who are deviant. Pupils, however, are subject to another series of controls: control by the informal social order.

The introduction of the term informal social order raises a crucial distinction which runs throughout the rest of this manual. This distinction is between the *formal social order* and the *informal social order* and we repeat the definitions of these concepts:

> *Formal social order*: Norms, values and relationships prescribed structurally or normatively by the goal system.
>
> *Informal social order*: Norms, values and relationships not prescribed structurally or normatively by the goal system but which may have functions for it.

In other words, the formal order is the 'official' one and some aspects of it have been discussed in the previous chapters on goals and subunits. The informal social order is a dynamic force in the world of the groups within the school, staff and pupils, and consists of rules, standards and controls members exercise over one another.

All adults and children in the school are controlled by informal social norms. We shall concentrate here on the informal order of the pupils and the way pupils control other pupils.

The two orders may be congruent to varying degrees. Sometimes they are opposed, for example in schools where pupils have an unwritten rule which is strictly enforced, saying 'never speak unnecessarily to staff' or 'don't show any enthusiasm for anything outside the classroom', whereas the formal order tries to encourage close staff-pupil relations or extracurricular activities. The relationships between the two systems will be discussed in chapter IV.

5 Informal control

(i) Informal assimilation processes Previously we examined assimilation into the formal social order. Assimilation into the informal social order consists largely of the norms senior staff and pupils have for dealing with newcomers. These norms may approve or sanction methods of assimilation, such as making new children mix with one age group or bullying them. These methods may not be specifically sanctioned by the school rules but they are closely controlled by private pupil rules which advise, 'keep to your own age group'. Deviance from this prescription is sanctioned by the methods of informal control analysed at the end of this section (p. 116).

Many of these methods may be known to staff, others may not. The policy the staff take is one example of the relationship between the formal and informal orders which is to be discussed in chapter IV. They may encourage or forbid certain informal methods or choose to tolerate minor abuses rather than antagonise important informal groups.

Nine methods of assimilation are described. Again it must be repeated that these methods are in the *informal* social order, not the formal.

This distinction betwen formal and informal assimilation processes adds clarity to discussions on aspects such as the *length of the assimilation process*. Supposing you ask 'when is a new pupil no longer new?' The time as defined by the formal order may differ from that of the pupils' informal world. The formal processes may end abruptly with promotion at the end of term while informal processes such as nicknames may last longer.

(i) Informal assimilation processes

NORMS:	(a) Period when norms are not applied to new pupils
	(b) Period when informal norms are more rigorous for new pupils
REACTIONS OF OLDER PUPILS:	(a) General helpfulness to new pupils
	(b) Tough approach; reserve towards new pupils, bullying
INTERNAL ASSOCIATIONS:	(a) Restrictions on association with other pupils.
	(b) Association with other pupils encouraged
MEMBERSHIP:	(a) Restrictions on membership of teams, societies for new pupils
	(b) New pupils encouraged to stick to own (junior) societies and teams
PRIVILEGES:	(a) New boys accorded special informal privileges
	(b) Informal rights and privileges withheld from new pupils
INSIGNIA:	(a) Insignia to distinguish new pupils
NICKNAMES:	(a) Use of customs, nicknames for new pupils
RITUALS:	(a) Rituals associated with ending of assimilation
RELATIONS WITH HOME:	(a) Encouraged to see parents, to write, etc., sympathy to homesickness
(for residential schools only)	(b) Discouraged to see, talk about parents, mockery of homesickness

(ii) Informal rewards and sanctions Informal rewards and sanctions are those which pupils (or staff) exercise over one another. Again our typology is best suited to the pupils' informal social order. We classify the controls the same way as we classified formal controls into coercive, utilitarian and normative kinds.

The strength and pervasiveness of these informal controls will depend to some degree, on the nature of formal controls. The more prevalent coercive control in goal areas the wider the gap will be between the formal order and the pupils' informal order. The more prevalent formal normative control, the narrower the gap will be.

(ii) Informal rewards and sanctions

SANCTIONS

Coercive:	Violence, bullying
Utilitarian:	Removal of some amenity or facility of no status value, e.g. books
Normative:	Verbal, use of surname, sarcasm
	Ostracism, sending to coventry
	Insignia, symbols
	Type-grouping, nicknames

REWARDS

Coercive:	By definition cannot exist
Utilitarian:	Accommodation
	Food
	Dress
	Service, fagging
Normative:	Insignia
	Social privileges
	Competition
	Nicknames
	Group loyalty

6 Summary of controls

Lastly, we summarise the types of control employed to counteract deviance in different goal areas. This provides a useful framework for comparing control processes in different kinds of school.

This chapter has analysed control in the widest sense. Some of the controls, such as rewards and sanctions, are easily analysed from interviews (headmaster q.3; housemaster q.2; head of school q.2) which are crosschecked by pupils' writings on punishments they have received recently. However, in discussions on control too much emphasis is often put on rewards and sanctions as the sole means of control. The chapter demonstrates that there are other important mechanisms of control and various types have been discussed. Some of these are easily analysed, for example structural controls over office, which are readily assessed from the headmaster's interview (qq.3, 8, 11), though other controls are less easy to investigate systematically as the processes are so intangible. Control by orientation to expressive ends, for example, is very important but the attempts to reduce it to a measuring scale (p. 324) fall very short of a satisfactory analysis as the inherent weaknesses of all measuring scales are increased by the social-psychological nature of the process which this one attempts to measure.

Nevertheless, some useful material comes from pupil interviews and replies to questions on starting school (qq.27-30) for processes like assimilation and certain norms (q.89) on treating new pupils are relevant.

To analyse other modes or orientations to goal attainment, a combination of interviewing and participant observation is needed. Some information, such as the use of competition in the academic sphere, can be collected when interviewing staff about the academic subunit, but observation of rituals, traditions, culture and taste presented to pupils are equally important. The questions about the qualities of leavers (headmaster q.19; housemaster q.17) and on success in goal attainment (headmaster q.18; housemaster q.16) give a useful insight into the ends to which this control is oriented and it is useful to bear these ends in mind in later interviews.

Informal control among pupils is more easily analysed from the informal control questions p. 293 and questions 72, 74, 75, 77, 89, on the informal system in the main questionnaire. Informal assimilation is obtained from these same questions as well as questions 27, 28, 29, 30 (parents interview qq.34-41) on starting school.

6 Summary of controls

GOAL AREAS	CONTROLS EMPLOYED BY FORMAL SOCIAL ORDER				CONTROLS EMPLOYED BY INFORMAL SOCIAL ORDER	
	Structural control over office	Rewards and Sanctions	Institutional Control	Orientation to goal attainment	Informal Control	Coercive/Utilitarian/Normative
INSTRUMENTAL						
EXPRESSIVE						
ORGANISATIONAL						

7 Bibliography

The following texts are relevant to the chapter on control:
B. Bernstein 1967; S. M. Dornbusch 1955; A. Etzioni 1962; R. Farley 1960; B. J. Georgopolous 1958; M. E. Highfield 1952; L. M. McCorkle 1954; M. Punch 1966, 1967; S. Wheeler 1961; N. M. Zald 1963.

IV Adaptation and the informal social order

We have seen how the organisation sets itself goals and prosecutes them through the subunits and how mechanisms of control are used. This chapter looks at the response of pupils and staff to these goals and the means of control.

Their adaptation are examined using the general paradigm of Robert K. Merton and then related to a wider informal social order and one of its important components—the underculture.

Five examples follow of situations where adaptations are closely controlled by the informal order. These are all examples of social interaction or sexual adaptation. It should be emphasised that these patterns of adaptation are controlled largely by the informal order whatever the formal order may prescribe.

Indeed, the orientation of the informal order to the formal order is a crucial relationship, for where the informal norms are hostile to certain goals (e.g. in academic or cultural areas) then the effectiveness of the organisation is much reduced.

We first look at the way pupils of different ages and abilities respond to the expectations of the formal order.

1 Adaptation to the society

The five possible responses are based on the paradigm of R. K. Merton which suggests that responses to any social structure can be classified by examining whether or not the goals and the approved means of achieving them are accepted.*

Conformity is acceptance of a goal and the institutionalised means of achieving the goal.

Ritualism is non-acceptance of a goal but acceptance of the institutionalised means of achieving the goal.

Retreatism is non-acceptance of both a goal and the institutionalised means of achieving it.

Innovation is acceptance of a goal but non-acceptance of the institutionalised means of achieving it.

Rebellion is rejection of a goal and institutionalised means of achieving it and replacement with others goals and means.

Two features of the responses are analysed: the *extent* of the adaptation (i.e. the proportion of people adapting in a particular way) and the *degree* of adaptation (i.e. the depth to which the adaptation is taken up), by various age groups and by streams within age groups, since the adaptation patterns of able children can differ markedly from those of the less able.

Adaptations are analysed for six areas: authority, athletic, academic, social, religious, cultural.

Each area is relevant to a question on the social adaptation test which is given in the methodology. The extent of adaptation is easily measured from the social adaptation test (below p. 295). The degree of adaptation, however, is more difficult to assess and information may only be forthcoming for a few adaptations and areas, (e.g. pupil q.87 for the authority area, housemaster interview q.13).

* J. Wakeford in *The Cloistered Elite* (Macmillan, 1969) has usefully extended the Mertonian range of adaptations by his concept of ' colonisation '.

1 Adaptation to the society

In Areas
Authority Athletic Academic Social Religious Cultural

CONFORMITY extent

RITUALISM extent

RETREATISM extent

INNOVATION extent

REBELLION extent

Examine for age groups
  (i) First year, each stream
  (ii) 'O' level year, each stream
  (iii) Sixth form

Assess the *degree* of response if possible

Relate adaptations to the main *goals* which the above subsystems serve

ADAPTATION TO GOALS

Adaptation	Instrumental	Expressive	Organisational
(extent or degree)			
Conformity			
Ritualism			
Retreatism			
Innovation			
Rebellion			

An index or score can be devised for the extent of adaptation by examining the proportions choosing the various responses.

Once such data is analysed the resulting scores for each adaptation can be related to the goal areas served by the subsystem (e.g. conformity to instrumental ends and means may be accompanied in some schools by conformity to expressive ends and means but in other schools by ritualism or rebellion or innovation). Such an analysis is profoundly useful for comparing the effect of different schools.

After this general analysis we can relate kinds of pupil adaptations, deviant or committed, to the kinds of control discussed in the preceding chapter.

2   Adaptations to control

We can now relate the main modes of adaptation found among pupils to the basic kinds of control found in schools. We express this in terms of a dimension ranging from control which is predominantly coercive at one end, to that which is predominantly normative at the other.

The more control tends to be coercive—whether generally in the school, in one of its subunits, or goal areas—then the more widespread and intense will be deviance from its ends and means, and the less there will be of commitment to them. *Deviant* adaptations will consist principally of rebellion, retreatism and ritualism. *Committed* ones will include little conformity. In fact, the nearest committed response will be innovation: those who accept the goals but wish to change the coercive means.

The more normative controls are adopted, the more the pattern of deviance and commitment alters. Where normative control predominates, commitment will be widespread and deviance will be less widespread (though it may be intense). *Committed* adaptation will consist in conformity: that is acceptance of both the ends and means of the school. Chief among *deviant* adaptations will be innovation—a desire to change current means. (In coercive situations, innovation is the most likely committed response, in norma-

2   Adaptations to control

Where coercive control predominates:
   Deviance will be widespread and intense
      Main modes: Rebellion (widespread and intense)
                    Ritualism (widespread)
                    Retreatism (widespread not intense)
   Commitment will be scarce and low
      Main modes: Innovation (the nearest committed response
                              widespread, not intense)
Where normative control predominates:
   Commitment will be widespread and intense
      Main mode: conformity (widespread and intense)
   Deviance will be less widespread and less intense
      Main modes: Innovation (now a deviant response, widespread
                              and intense)
                Ritualism (may be widespread)
                Retreatism (not widespread but intense)
                Rebellion (not widespread but may be intense)

tive ones it is the most likely deviant response.) Ritualism and retreatism follow in the same order, and rebellion is the least widespread response (it is the most widespread deviant response in coercive situations). Rebellious adaptation can be intense, however, towards both coercive control, which is usually crude and obvious, and the normative kind, which can produce intense hostility because of its encompassing flexibility and subtlety: some pupils experience it more as a stranglehold than is the case with coercive control. Likewise, normative controls engender a deeper withdrawal from them than do coercive controls because they are more difficult to escape. Though retreatism may be common in predominantly coercive school situations, it may be less intense than in normative situations.

We now turn from the adaptations of individual pupils to those of their informal social order as a whole.

3 The informal social order

We now reach one of the most important sections of this manual: *the informal social order,* or the interrelationships that grow up in the operation of the society.

This has been defined earlier as ' norms, values and relationships not laid down by the goal system even though they may have functions (or dysfunctions) for it '. The informal social order does not necessarily pursue goals, it exercises functions not performed by the formal social order. These functions may oppose, supplement or complement the formal order.

Now we will discuss the informal social order itself.

(i) Means which the informal social order employs Section 1: Examines the means the informal order uses to ensure conformity to its demands. This was analysed in the sections on informal social controls and so is not dealt with here (see above p. 112).

(ii) Relationship between the formal and informal social orders Section 2: Is crucial to the operation of the school. It deals with the nature of the relationship between the formal and informal orders.

Four relationships are described. The formal order may be *unaware* of the informal order's existence or some of its processes or practices. In contrast, it may decide to *tolerate* its standards or attempt to ignore the more overt manifestations (such as unwillingness to support school functions). Occasionally it may even *manoeuvre* leaders in the informal order either to assist discipline, inculcate official values or further its ends, for example, by using bullies to keep order or by giving charismatic leaders high formal offices. Finally, the formal order may attempt to *suppress* aspects of the life and operation of the informal one.

3 The informal social order

(i) Means which the informal social order employs
Classified under section on informal social controls (p. 112).

(ii) Relationships between the formal and the informal orders
   (a) IGNORANT: Existence of informal system unrecognised
   (b) TOLERANT: Aware of existence but blind eye turned to its manifestations or put up with
   (c) MANIPULATIVE: Deliberate use of co-operation in order to further ends, channel information, help control
   (d) SUPPRESSIVE: Attempt to suppress the informal order

(iii), (iv) Orientation and integration Sections (iii) and (iv) examine the orientation and integration of the two social orders. The orientation to formal norms, roles, authority and change are examined in section (iii). The degree of integration of the two orders is examined in section (iv) for the eight basic areas of school life.

(v) Pervasiveness Section (v) is a summary of the pervasiveness or strength and homogeneity of the content of the informal social order. It asks: which system do the pupils live under most of all? Is the informal social order closely linked with the formal or are they two different worlds which call for a double life from the pupils? Is the informal order strong or can pupils escape its demands and sanctions? By 'homogeneity of the informal order' we mean that its norms are homogeneous whether or not they are supportive of the formal order or antagonistic to it. Again different schools produce markedly different kinds of informal orders with powerful effects on their success in attaining goals.

It may appear difficult to gather data relevant for this section. In practice it is not difficult, as so much data is relevant. Interviews with staff, and pupils' writings and diaries are all relevant. The questions on norms (q.89), informal control and underlife are important, as are the questions on staff attempts to change the informal order (head boy interviews, housemaster qq.10, 11; headmaster qq.7, 9, 10), as so often the informal order blocks successful implementation of changes desired by the formal order.

The pervasiveness or inescapability of the order is examined by the informal control questions and the strength of norms q.86 (numerical frequency count). The orientation of the system can be found by comparing formally approved behaviour (e.g. housemaster qq.12, 15, 13, 17) with informal norms q.89, aspirations q.85, popular, unpopular qq.74, 75 and 72 and q.77. Also the staff-pupil relations test is relevant.

The effects of the strength and character of the informal order and its relationship with the formal order is one of the key variables between schools and has a profound influence on the workings of any school. The relevant hypotheses are 1, 10, 14, 27, 30, 31, 32, 33, 39, 43, 45 and 60-69.

We have observed that informal social orders with little consensus on norms may cohere at crisis moments when both formal and informal order are forced to define their positions. Such

(iii) Orientation of informal social order

Orientation of informal social order to:	*AWAY FROM FORMAL ORDER*	*TOWARDS FORMAL ORDER*
Formal norms:		
Stated goals:	(a) Instrumental	
	(b) Expressive	
	(c) Organisational	
Formally approved changes		
Formal roles: Staff		
Pupil		
Formal authority: Staff		
Pupil		

(iv) Scope of integration of formal and informal orders in areas

Area	*Senior Pupils*	*Junior Pupils*
Organisation, routine	Assess for each whether:	
Social, recreative	(a) The informal order is highly	
Academic	integrated with the formal	
Cultural, creative	order	
Religious, ethical	(b) The informal order is separate	
Administrative	from the formal order	
Athletic		
Pastoral		

(v) Summary: Pervasiveness of the informal social order

(a) All-pervasive, norms homogeneous (whether supportive or hostile to formal order)
(b) Pervasive, but norms are heterogeneous
(c) Not pervasive, but norms are homogeneous
(d) Not pervasive, but norms are heterogeneous

moments can occur after a period of license by the formal order as tighter control is reintroduced and there follows not only significant changes in the strength of norms but even in the norms themselves. These trigger points at which informal norms may change can give insights into the problem of how norms originate and change although a systematic approach is difficult to carry through.

We now look at five manifestations of the informal social order—pupil taste, staff associations, staff-pupil relations, pupil associations and sexual adaptations.

4 Examples

(i) Example 1: Pupil taste One manifestation of the pupil informal social order is the musical and literary taste of the pupils. This is an adaptation to culture goals which are one particular type of expressive goals. The varieties of adaptation demonstrate how the informal order of the pupils can reinforce or counteract prescriptions of the formal social order. Details of the background of the pupils, the nature of the cultural goals and the relationship between the formal and· informal social orders should be taken into account in any extended analysis of this adaptation.

(ii) Example 2: Staff associations This section takes into account the informal order by which the staff are controlled and examines the norms governing relationships among staff. The quality of associations and the basic factors influencing them are considered first. The final summary examines the formal and informal norms controlling associations among staff. There may be a conflict here between the prescriptions of the two orders. The formal order may discourage close relationships between senior and young staff while the informal order may encourage the opposite. There is likely to be a difference in the norms governing *vertical* associations which are associations between staff in different status positions from the norms governing *horizontal* relationships which are associations among staff of similar status positions. The headmaster's relationship with his staff is also important here because this is influenced

4   Examples

(i)   Example 1: Pupil taste

Music and Reading	Examine for:
Taste supported by pupil informal order	Junior, Middle, and Senior pupils
Taste formally approved by school	
Support of pupil norms on taste for cultural goals of school	

(ii)   Example 2: Staff association

(a)   *Quality of staff associations*
      Homogeneous and friendly
      Homogeneous but reserved
      Divisions exist but not antagonistic
      Antagonistic divisions

(b)   *Factors influencing staff associations*
Examine the extent to which staff associations are influenced by:
      Age
      Status
      Subject
      Sex

by staff norms which may discourage a close relationship whatever good intentions the headmaster may have.

Having looked at staff associations we now look at staff-pupil relations.

(iii) Example 3: Staff-pupil relations The norms of the informal order of both staff and pupils govern the relationships that can develop between the official world and the pupils. Here we illustrate the nature of the relations possible between the formal and informal orders, what sort of contact the informal norms will permit. It provides a further example of informal normative influence on behaviour.

(a) *The nature of relations*: This section assesses how close in fact are the relations between pupils and staff. It considers the intimacy likely in contacts with pupils of various ages, and estimates the quality of contact, close or distant, which various staff roles may involve. For example it is likely that staff-prefect contact will be close in organisational matters, and that the successful playing of a pastoral role could depend on a closer relationship than that necessary for academic roles.

(c) *Norms influencing staff association*

| | Patterns of staff association approved by: |
Formal Social Order	Staff Informal Social Order
	State whether the relationships permitted are:
Vertical association	distant
Horizontal association	reserved, with small friendship groups
Headmaster-Staff relations	close

(iii) Example 3: Staff-pupil relations

(a) *The nature of relations*

Assess thus: (1) Generally distant, official, master-pupil
(2) Mixed, partly official, partly close
(3) Generally close, casual friendly, man to
man

	Staff Roles		
	Instrumental	Expressive	Organisational
	1 2 3 4 5	6 7 8 9 10 11 12	13 14 15 16 17 18

Nature of staff relations with:
Prefects
Sixth form   Classify for nature of staff-pupil relations
Fifth form   for each age group and each staff role
Third form
First form

(b), (c) *Control by pupils over their relations with staff*: However, it is realised that the requirements for successful role performance and what the informal order may permit can be very different. Here we analyse the control exercised by the pupils over the relations with the staff and the control which the informal norms of the staff may exert over staff members in their relations with the pupils.

A disparity between the two systems in this area has far reaching consequences for many other areas, especially goals, and adaptation to the structure.

This section is crucial to an understanding of the informal social order as so many pupil norms (q.89) include strict codes of behaviour for dealing with staff. In some cases the encouragement of casual friendly relations by the formal order is blocked in practice by pupil norms that are against casual friendly association with staff.

A great deal of data can be obtained here: from interviews with staff (housemaster qq.2, 3, 13) and pupils, much from pupils' writings (qq.13, 14, 89, 82, 81, 79, 80) and the staff-pupil relations test.

After examining staff-pupil relations we now look at pupil associations.

(iv) Example 4: Patterns of pupil association This section deals with patterns of association among pupils. A pattern of association means in this context: 'a voluntary and mutual interaction in which neither party plays any role associated with an authority position'.

Thus a prefect reprimanding a young offender is *not* a pattern of association, but a prefect playing a private game of chess with a younger pupil is a mutual association.

Two kinds of association are discussed: that permitted by the formal order and that permitted by the informal order.

For each, the association may be vertical (between pupils of different age groups) or horizontal (between subunits of pupils of similar age groups).

Some schools have rules about association—usually vertical association—so the relationships permitted by the formal order can easily be found from interviews and examination of rules.

(b) *Control by pupils over their relations with staff*

	FORMAL			INFORMAL		
	Permits Official Only	Permits Casual Friendly	Encourages Casual Friendly	Permits Official Only	Permits Casual Friendly	Encourages Casual Friendly
Senior Pupils						
Junior Pupils, all streams						

(c) *Control by staff over their relations with pupils*

	FORMAL			INFORMAL		
	Permits Official Only	Permits Casual Friendly	Encourages Casual Friendly	Permits Official Only	Allows Casual Friendly	Encourages Casual Friendly
PUPILS						
Sixth						
Fifth, all streams						
Juniors, all streams						

(iv) Example 4: Patterns of pupil association

(a) *Patterns of association permitted by the formal order*

(1) VERTICAL ASSOCIATION: Between pupils of different age groups and sexes

(2) HORIZONTAL ASSOCIATION: Between subunits of pupils of similar ages and between sexes

SUBUNIT 1	*SUBUNIT 2*	
Seniors	Seniors	Mark with directed arrows e.g. for permitted formal association
Middle	Middle	
Juniors	Juniors	

The informal order may discourage young pupils from associating with older pupils or from associating with pupils in other forms or houses. Sometimes norms give clear orders 'never make friends with older boys', 'stick to your own year for friends'. On other occasions the opposite is true: 'be friendly to all pupils in other forms or houses' or 'get a big boy to protect you'; so in these cases the informal order permits wide friendships (often when the formal order does everything possible to prevent them). Similarly with girl-boy relationships, whatever the formal rules may say about association, the informal order may prescribe strict codes by which an older boy is permitted to associate with a younger girl but not an older girl with a younger boy and the actual age range of such associations may be carefully prescribed and controlled. Besides such vertical controls, it may also prescribe broader horizontal ones, the degree to which it is socially imperative to have a girl friend or it is socially acceptable to be without one and at what age.

The evidence for the relationships permitted by the informal order comes mainly from norms questions 89, and questions on close friendships. The evidence for relationships permitted by the formal order comes from interviews with staff and boys and girls (for unwritten formal rules) and written rules.

Probably one of the most significant areas controlled by the informal social order are our next examples: the heterosexual and homosexual adaptations of the pupils.

(v) Example 5: Sexual adaptations In residential schools an important example of pupil adaptations and, in some cases of under-culture, is the sexual adaptation of the pupils. Much of this section can be applied to day schools too for relations within the school or its precincts.

(a) *Heterosexual relations*: This section examines the heterosexual adaptation of the pupils.

The first part analyses the heterosexual relationships permitted by the formal order (i.e. relationships officially approved by school) in four areas.

After this comes the types of relationships controlled by the informal order (i.e. pupil norms). The formal order may be aware of this or not: or it may be tolerant, manipulative or suppressive. The relationship between the two systems was analysed earlier.

(b) *Patterns of association permitted by the informal order*

   (1) VERTICAL ASSOCIATION: By age and sex

   (2) HORIZONTAL ASSOCIATION: By age and sex

SUBUNIT 1	*SUBUNIT 2*	
Seniors	Seniors	Mark with directed arrows relations permitted by the informal order
Middle	Middle	
Juniors	Juniors	

(v) **Example 5: Sexual adaptations**

   (a) *Heterosexual relations*
      Relations permitted by formal order
         Academic
         Cultural
         Social, dances, etc.
         Personal, individual
      Relations permitted by informal order
         Meeting girls/boys regularly
         Having girl/boy friend
         Emotional involvement
         Physical sexual involvement

The second section examines the types of heterosexual activity found in the school. It is very important for clear argument on this controversial topic to distinguish mere social interaction with the opposite sex (i.e. meeting girls) from emotional involvement and from *physical* sexual involvement.

The third section examines the modes of control by the formal and informal orders over formal and informal heterosexual relations. The formal controls (i.e. official policy) can prohibit, supervise or neglect while informal controls can suppress, tolerate or approve.

(v)   Example 5 (cont.): Homosexuality This section examines homosexual relationships between pupils and applies principally to single sex residential schools.

Four types of homosexuality are distinguished and these should be analysed for three age group categories—between junior and junior pupils, senior and senior pupils and senior and junior pupils.

The next section deals with the controls over homosexuality. This is extremely important, as homosexual activity is controlled mostly by the *informal* order. If pupil norms support homosexual activity, it will occur whatever the attitude of the formal order, though if the formal order is greatly suppressive it will go underground.

The formal policy is divided into suppression, manipulation and tolerance. School stated policy and actual policy on this matter are distinguished as different, as few schools have a stated tolerant policy. 'Manipulation' is a midway policy by which the formal order does not necessarily approve of homosexual behaviour but tolerates it so as to improve its effectiveness in other areas (e.g. pastoral, discipline). Informal control by the pupils themselves too can be suppressive, tolerant or fashionable; in the

(b) *Types of heterosexual activity*
    Meeting girls/boys regularly
    Emotional involvement
    Physical sexual involvement

(c) *Modes of control over heterosexual relations*

Formal Relations	*Formal Control*			*Informal Control*		
	Prohibited	Supervised	Little Supervised	Suppressive	Tolerant	Fashionable
Academic						
Cultural						
Social—dances						
Personal—individual						
Informal Relations						
Meeting girls/boys regularly						
Have girl/boy friend						
Emotional involvement						
Physical sexual involvement						

(v) Example 5 (cont.): Homosexuality

(a) *Types of homosexuality present*

		Between Pupils	
	Junior-Junior	Senior-Junior	Senior-Senior
(1) Physical experimentation (juniors only)			
(2) Emotional relations solely			
(3) Emotional *and* physical relations			
(4) Physical relations solely			

(b) *Modes of control over homosexual activity*

	MODES OF CONTROL	
Formal	*Manipulative*	*Informal*
(1) Policy Suppressive		(i) Suppressive
(2) Actually Suppressive		(ii) Tolerant
(3) Policy Tolerant		(iii) Fashionable
(4) Actually Tolerant		

latter situation the pupil norms make it 'the done thing' and award its practicers with high informal status.

A summary follows: the collective orientation of the school.

Obviously material for this section is sensitive and secret. A good assessment is obtained by questions on the questionnaire on advantages/disadvantages of single sex schooling, (q.57) of what school promotes (q.86), what makes a boy popular/unpopular (qq.74, 75) and norms (q.89).

Accurate statistical indication of the orientation of the school towards homosexuality and heterosexuality can come from 'Picture Tests' (Thematic Apperception Tests) which have proved a sensitive guide to these situations.

Once the observer has gained the confidence of the pupils, he will find frank discussion of the topic in pupil diaries, and can pursue the topic in conversation with staff and informal chats with groups of senior pupils.

Again, this is an area of activity strictly controlled by the *informal* order. If the norms of the informal order deem such behaviour fashionable, there is very little the formal order can do, other than complete suppression, to prevent it (see the discussion in Lambert, 1968).

We have looked at the goals, subunits and mechanisms of orientation and control and have examined the response of the individuals to them. These sociological and social psychological aspects are linked in the next section on roles, for a role is not only prescribed by the structure but is also interpreted by the role player.

5 Bibliography

The following texts are relevant to the chapter on adaptation and the informal social order:
Adaptation:

E. A. Allen 1961; R. Barton 1959; F. Bodman 1950; M. Castle 1954; R. A. Cloward 1959; A. K. Cohen 1967; R. R. Dale 1965; R. Dubin 1959; R. K. Merton 1957, 1959; T. M. Newcomb 1943; J. Wakeford 1969; J. Withall 1952.

(c) *Summary: Collective orientation of informal order*
(1) Heterosexual
(2) Heterosexual but homosexual fringe
(3) Largely homosexual

Staff World:
P. Lambert 1958.

Staff-Pupil Relations:
H. S. Becker 1953; M. Shipman 1967; J. Webb 1962.

Pupil-Pupil Relations:
W. A. L. Blyth 1958, 1960; D. S. Cartwright 1961; J. S. Coleman 1961; K. M. Evans 1962; C. W. Gordon 1957; S. Kosofsky 1958; J. L. Moreno 1960; H. W. Polsky 1962; L. Ridgway 1965.

The Informal Social System:
H. S. Becker 1961; B. B. Berk 1966; D. Cressey 1958; J. S. Coleman 1960; D. Clemmer 1958; F. M. Ellkin 1946; C. A. Ford 1929; R. Giallombardo 1966; E. Goffman 1961; O. Grusky 1959; D. H. Hargreaves 1967; I. Harper 1952; R. Lambert 1968; T. M. Newcomb 1967; C. Shrag 1954; B. Sugarman 1967; G. M. Sykes 1958, 1960; P. H. Taylor 1962; D. A. Ward 1964, 1965.

V Roles

If goals are to be realised, tasks must be divided among the members of the social system. Roles are allocated to individuals who usually carry related status and authority. So each role-player has a role set, 'that complement of role relationships in which persons are involved by virtue of occupying a particular social status', which is ordained by the formal order. However, his performance is influenced by his own evaluation of the primacy of certain roles and by his status in the *informal* social order.

Thus in any role set, certain roles may not be compatible (e.g. pastoral and disciplinary roles). The roles may be said to conflict.

These role sets must cohere into a viable overall role structure. But the analysis is further complicated by the fact that this structure itself builds in conflicts, examples of which are given in the text. So that although an individual may have a perfectly compatible role set, in the structural context he may suffer role conflicts. The greater the structural role conflict, the less effective will be the organisation in achieving its goals.

1   Role distribution in the school

A role may be defined as: 'the legitimately expected behaviour of persons in the social system'.

This first section examines the *distribution* of roles in the school. It asks, do key members of major subunits (like housemasters) exercise major roles in other major subunits such as those of careers master or head of department?

Three *types of distribution* are given:

(i) *Parallel*:   Where functions in the subunit are structurally separate from main function in other subunits (e.g. housemaster cannot be head of department).

(ii) *Mixed*:   Where there is some separation but not total separation.

(iii) *Integrated*:   Where there is no structural separation between major roles in different subunits.

As with goals, a great deal of data is collected which is relevant to this section. All the interviews examine roles in depth and the role sheet assesses both role satisfaction and role conflicts.

1 Role distribution in the school

(i) Parallel
(ii) Mixed
(iii) Integrated

2   Staff roles

After gleaning information from staff interviews (headmaster qq. 2, 3, 4; housemaster qq.2, 3) and role sheets, an assessment can be made of an individual's performance in each of eighteen roles. This delineates the individual's role set—' that complement of role relationships in which persons are involved by virtue of occupying a particular social status '.

The roles are divided into the same categories as goals—instrumental, expressive and organisational—so the two can be related.

Two dimensions are analysed here:

(i) The degree to which the individual role-player sees and takes up his role.

(ii) The degree to which the formal social order *expects* the individual role-player to take up that role.

The information for the first comes from interviews, the second from the role sheet and from the headmaster's interviews (qq.2, 3, 4). Many cross-checks can be used. For example, pupils' replies to the questions on taking problems to staff (qq.65, 66, 67) is a check on the actual pastoral role of the staff.

In some schools, particularly residential ones, senior pupils play certain staff roles, especially organisational ones. They are included here with the list of staff.

2 Staff roles (Examined in terms of the goals to which they are directed)

Instrumental:
  Academic
  Vocational guidance
  Social training, manners, etc.
  Citizenship, duty to community
  Physical training and development

Expressive:
  Religious functions
  Ethical exemplar
  Cultural
  Personal and pastoral
  Encouraging sportsmanship
  Homely
  Encouraging self discipline

Organisational:
  Control, order, discipline
  Filling in time, keeping pupils occupied
  Domestic duties
  Continuity of organisation over time, admissions, recruitment
  Servicing the organisation, administrative
  Maintaining organisation's reputation outside

ASSESS: (i) The degree to which the individual sees and takes up his role
         (ii) The degree to which the school expects the individual to take up the role
             (a) Governors
             (b) Headmaster
             (c) Senior Master
             (d) Housemaster
             (e) Form master
             (f) Heads of Departments
             (g) Chaplain
             (h) Boarding staff
             (i) Teaching staff
             (j) Bursar
             (k) Domestic staff
             (l) Bureaucratic staff

3 Role definition

This section summarises the degree to which the roles are laid down. For example, extracurricular duties may be clearly laid down by a contract, laid down by informal prescription or simply defined by the norms of the society. In this last case the role-player just waits to see what is expected of him in certain situations as he internalises the norms of the society.

4 Summary: The nature of the staff role structure

The role structure for the staff of the school can be summarised by combining the role distribution (section 1) with the staff role patterns (section 2).

There are three kinds of role distribution—parallel, mixed and integrated and three kinds of role patterns:

Multiple roles: Most staff play instrumental, expressive and organisational roles

Mixed roles: Most staff play instrumental, and organisational roles, a few staff play expressive roles

Simple roles: Most staff play instrumental and organisational roles or organisational roles only

Roles could also be classified in the same way as goals, where a typology was constructed based on the dominance of instrumental, expressive or organisational goals. Details can be found in the relevant section.

These analyses give us a view of the total role structure and the role sets of particular individuals. It would be wrong to assume, however, that all these are compatible and mutually supporting for, as the next section will show, role sets and role structures are subject to inbuilt conflicts.

(m) Other (specify)
Pupils
(a) Head of school
(b) Head of house
(c) Prefect
(d) Sixth former

3 Role definition

Are staff roles: (i)   Prescribed formally
(ii) Prescribed informally
(iii) Indefinite

4 Summary: The nature of the staff role structure

                    ROLE DISTRIBUTION
                         Parallel   Mixed   Integrated
ROLE PATTERNS
Multiple roles
Mixed roles
Simple roles

5   Role conflict

Types of role conflict:

Four types are used here:

Conflicts in individual role sets: Where roles within a particular role set conflict for some reason.

(i)   *Time-energy conflict*: Where the role-player has insufficient time or energy or resources to play all roles to the level of his own and others' expectations. A common situation for housemasters—running house and teaching, etc.

(ii)   *Conflict between roles*: (a) *Roles for one status position*: Where the expectations of actors interacting with the role player conflicts because of the nature of his role set. For example, a housemaster who has to be chief disciplinary and chief pastoral agent for pupils in his house. (b) *Roles for several status positions*: Where an individual holding several statuses has to reconcile the demands of the various membership groups to which he belongs (e.g. a housemaster who has a family).

Although an individual's role set may be free from conflict, there will be other role-players whose role sets overlap with his. This leads to conflict which is inherent in the structure and cannot be resolved by any individual role-player working alone.

Conflicts of role structure: Where conflicts arise from interaction between different individuals with overlapping role sets.

(iii)   *Conflict within one role among different role-players*: Where two or more role-players play the same roles but the prescription of the roles is not sufficiently precise to prevent duplication. For example, the headmaster and bursar may both have administrative powers. Both may legally issue different directives for some occasion (e.g. end of term) or event, and it may require consultation to sort things out. Another example is between the duty master and prefects, both of whom have a role—say to supervise meals—but who may conflict (e.g. on the tolerable level of noise or movement).

5 Role conflict

TYPES OF ROLE CONFLICT
CONFLICTS IN INDIVIDUAL ROLE SETS

(i) CONFLICTS OVER TIME-ENERGY DEMANDS OF ROLES

(ii) CONFLICTS BETWEEN ROLES ASSUMED BY ONE PERSON

CONFLICTS OF ROLE STRUCTURE
(iii) CONFLICTS OF DIFFERENT PERFORMERS OF SIMILAR ROLES

(iv) *Conflict with different roles played by different people*:
(a) Where one individual status holder has to play roles mediating the compulsory demands of different role-players, e.g. a headmaster may have to reconcile the demands of parents, staff and boys. Parents may want hard work, staff may want more recreation or games. The headmaster is caught in the middle and has to reconcile the role interests. (b) Where conflicting roles as in type ii are played by different people. An example is found where an individual master may be making attempts to help a boy meet a problem (pastoral role) while another member of staff finds the boy smoking and canes him (disciplinary role), so undoing and conflicting with the role of the other master. Another example is when the games master wants a boy to train hard while his tutor puts pressure on the boy for not working hard enough.

Individual role conflicts are most likely to occur in role sets which combine expressive and organisational roles. Instrumental and organisational roles will not conflict to the same degree. Structural role conflicts may occur for any roles. However, they are more likely to occur for organisational roles because in organisational areas situations arise which call for immediate action. The authority covering the role performance may be insufficiently defined or there may be little time for consultation with other role-players (e.g. a sudden administrative problem, or a sudden disciplinary problem).

(iv) CONFLICTS BETWEEN PERFORMANCE OR DE-
MANDS OF DIFFERENT ROLE-PLAYERS

Assess for all role-players: (list before) conflicts predominating:

	CONFLICT	
ROLE SETS	*STRUCTURES*	
1 2	3 4	

Officers
(specify)

6   Solutions of role conflicts in individual role sets

How do role players resolve conflicts in their individual role sets? This can be assessed by comparing the role esteemed by the school with the role esteemed by the player.

This can be discovered mainly from the interviews and role sheet.

After analysing staff roles, we now turn to pupil roles.

6 Solutions of role conflicts in individual role sets

Role player:	Role preferred by formal order	Role preferred by actor
(specify)		
1		
2		
3 etc.		

7 Pupil roles

After the analysis of staff roles comes the study of pupil roles. In boarding schools these roles are nearly always far more complicated than in day schools. Prefects, for example, often have to supervise dormitory hours, prep, etc., and in Public Schools they often coach games and administer corporal punishment. Senior pupils were included in the staff role analysis because some senior pupils take over several staff roles (e.g. discipline, administration); for a wider range of pupils a different framework is needed.

The pupil roles are divided into eight areas: for each area there are between two and four types ranging from mere participation or membership to directing.

Membership roles involve receiving the decisions or orders of others or generally participating.

Responsibility roles involve making decisions or administering decisions. In other words, roles are similar to those usually played by staff.

Assessment of the roles played by pupils at different ages— the four stages of their career described—should show how the roles change as a pupil moves up the school.

Most of the information for this section comes from the pupil interviews, housemaster and headmaster interviews, and the pupils' role sheet.

As we have said, roles are prescribed by the formal social order but this assumes that social conditions prevail which make the expected role performances possible. In exceptional conditions, either accidental or deliberate, the situations may change. An example of accidental change would be when a pupil takes up a staff role over others on a bus to quell disturbance.

Deliberate role reversal is termed *licence*. Licence is the informal toleration or formal approval of behaviour which is usually prohibited or sanctioned. Examples are critical sketches in house concerts, singing dirty songs on the rugger coach, role reversal at the end of term when seniors wait on juniors. At a different time or a different place this behaviour would be prohibited.

7 Pupil roles

Membership Responsibility roles

 (i) Academic
 (ii) Athletic
(iii) Discipline
(iv) Routine, organisation
 (v) Social unit
(vi) Cultural, creative
(vii) Administrative

Assess degree role taken up by pupils:

On entry to school
After two years in school
After five years in school
At top of school

8 Summary

(i) Complexity of pupils' roles The nature of the pupil role system can be summarised by combining the membership roles played with the staff or responsibility roles played.

The combination gives six types of pupil role. When the four stages of a pupil's career are considered, it gives another good guide to the change of roles with age, and between schools, it is a sensitive index to the different role patterns played by senior pupils.

(ii) Role conflict for pupils Role conflict for pupil officers can be analysed in the same way as for staff officers—by analysing conflicts of role sets and of role structures.

(iii) Solutions of role conflict The solution of role conflict for pupil officers can also be analysed in the same way as for staff.

The problem of role and goal conflicts raises the general sociological problem of the relationship between conflict and change.

Certainly some conflicts will act as a strong pressure for change (e.g. a radical difference in perception of real goals by fee-paying parents from that of the headmaster), though Coser has demonstrated that much conflict may merely help to maintain the status quo. Thus one of the conflicts described earlier (between the prescriptions of the formal and informal social orders regarding the nature of staff-pupil relations) is perpetuated in this way, for the more the formal order tries to exert its influence, the more the informal order resists and restores the previous state of affairs.

8 Summary

(i) Complexity of pupils' roles

Nature of Pupils' Roles:

Membership	Staff or Responsibility
(a) Limited	None
(b) Extensive	None
(c) Limited	Limited
(d) Extensive	Limited
(e) Extensive	Extensive
(f) Limited	Extensive

Plot the nature of the roles for pupils in each of four stages of their school career.

(ii) Role conflict for pupils

Role conflicts for pupils, plot as for staff

CONFLICTS

	Role sets		Role structures	
	1	2	3	4
Office				
(specify)				
1				
2				
3 etc.				

(iii) Solution of role conflict

	Role preferred by formal order	Role preferred by actor
Office		
1		
2		
3		

Most systematic material on roles comes from interviews in which role sets are examined (headmaster qq.2, 3; housemaster q.2; head boy qq.2, 3). Some assessment is also made of role satisfaction and evaluation (headmaster q.4; housemaster q.3). This material partly overcomes the problem that the analysis of roles has so many dimensions: what the person actually does, what he would like to do, what he feels he ought to do, what the organisation expects him to do and so on.

Numerical data which offer a rating of the roles performed and those expected from the role-player comes from the role sheet (p. 313). This avoids any of the complex qualifications which arise in interviews and offers a numerical index to analyse role sets. Though it obviously oversimplifies things, it proves a useful complement to the unco-ordinated details gathered from interviews. Only with a very general classification framework in mind (section 4) can all the material be handled, otherwise the process will be lost in a mass of detail. The classification we offer is very general and must be refined as evidence is sifted.

We now have a useful guide to the nature of staff role sets as well as the staff's evaluation and perception of their position. Many of the pupil responses check the role performance of staff. The replies to the pastoral care questions (qq.65, 66, 67), relations with staff (qq.13, 14, 68, 69), attitudes on religion and parental replies to contact with staff (q.30) assess the degree to which pupils reciprocate staff roles.

Pupil roles are less specific than staff roles and are more difficult to analyse from interviews (head of school qq.2, 3) because pupils take many aspects of their lives as given—they are not conscious of their roles. Again interview material and role sheet material offer a useful guide to the roles of senior pupils. Another technique, though very unsystematic, is to use pupil diaries. Here pupils present their roles clearly, although they think they are describing the daily round. This raises the problem of the reliability of individual material written by self-selected individuals. Diaries are useful if they complement other systematic material, but analysis which relies solely on this kind of material is not entirely adequate even if tremendous insights are demonstrated.

Role conflicts are widely discussed in sociology but it is extremely difficult to gather material on this topic. Interviews (headmaster q.5; housemaster q.4) do not yield very much, as respond-

ents are seldom conscious of all kinds of conflicts. The role sheet, which presents actual situations, is more useful, but even here the respondent may suddenly create examples without thinking if he had, in fact, been aware of such conflicts beforehand. Structural role conflicts, which we suggest are extremely important in determining the effectiveness of the school, are even more difficult to investigate, as they arise from interaction between role-players. Again interviews, role sheet answers and observation offer some guide, though evidence tends to be very patchy. Interviews exploring relationships between individuals are delicate and difficult to direct, while observation rests heavily on isolated incidents. We suggest that an exhaustive study of structural role conflict would be fruitful as this is one area where sociological concepts have completely outrun empirical methods.

9 Bibliography

The following texts are relevant to the chapter on roles:
C. R. Argyris 1959; M. Banton 1965; G. Bernbaum 1967; B. L. Bible 1963; B. J. Biddle 1961, 1966; C. E. Bidwell 1957; J. Floud 1962; C. E. Fishbourne 1962; A. G. Frank 1964; D. E. Gardner 1965; J. W. Getzels 1954, 1955; W. J. Goode 1958; N. Gross 1958, 1965; O. Grusky 1959; A. W. Halpin 1955, 1956; I. Harper 1952; D. J. Levinson 1959; R. K. Merton 1957; F. Musgrave 1965; D. Pugh 1966; M. Seeman 1953; S. Soles 1964; J. Toby 1952; J. P. Twyman 1963; C. Washbourne 1957; C. J. Westwood 1967, 1968; R. Wilkinson 1964; B. Wilson 1962.

VI Change

Change

There has been an attempt in previous areas to stress the conflict inherent in the social system of the school as well as the functional unity of various elements of the organisation. Thus, pressures for change may result from the conflicts, previously discussed in the sections on goals, roles and the informal social order, and which are to be discussed in the section on the relations of the schools with the wider society.*

Here we analyse the changes themselves. A distinction is made between structural and nonstructural change and, while mindful of the pressures inherent in the structure, attention is directed towards pressure groups and influential parasystems.

It is necessary to distinguish *three* kinds of change:

(i) *Changes in real goals:* These are defined as a change in the ends a school pursues in practice. Such changes can be long-term or short-term. A long-term change in real goals would occur for example, when a highly academic school had to alter some of its goals to cater for nonacademic children. Some changes can be short-term, usually cyclical in character, as when for several months a school may pursue a policy of strictness in discipline followed later by an easing up.

Long-term changes in real goals are fundamental and usually involve the second kind of change below.

(ii) *Changes in institutional structure*: This is defined as a change in the relationship between the school structure and its constituent parts: e.g. changes within and between these parts, changes in the system of status and authority, consciously planned changes in social composition, changes which substantially redefine the roles played by staff and pupils, changes in the relationship between the formal social order and the informal world of staff and pupils.

Examples of this would be the creation or abolition of tutor or house systems, or of academic departments, the creation of a careers officer, the creation of a school council.

(iii) *Changes which have no structural effect*: Nonstructural changes are those which are most numerous, as they do not substantially redefine the roles or authority of pupils or staff.

* see p. 193.

Examine changes that have taken place in the school *over last five years*
Distinguish throughout

(i) Changes in real goals of the school (a) permanent changes
(b) short-term changes in emphasis of real goals

(ii) Changes in the institutional structure of the school

(iii) Changes which involve *no* structural change

Examples could be new classrooms, alterations in curriculum, alteration of timetable, or privileges.

For each change the following features are then analysed:

(a) Area in which the change occurred.

(b) Process of decision-making and pressures for and against the change.

(c) The speed with which the change was accomplished.

(d) The effect of the change on roles.

1 Areas in which changes have occurred

The areas listed are the eight areas suggested earlier, which cover most aspects of school life.

No attempt is made to record the degree of change—i.e. whether profound or trivial.

1 Areas in which changes have occurred

    (i)   Organisation—Routine
   (ii)   Social—Recreative
  (iii)   Academic
  (iv)   Cultural—Creative
   (v)   Religious—Ethical
  (vi)   Administrative
 (vii)   Athletic
(viii)   Pastoral

2 Decision-making and sources of pressure for and against change

In any change the processes of pressure, influence and decision are all closely interrelated. Nevertheless certain areas can be separated clarifying comparisons and processes.

The *pressures* for or against change can be distinguished from the *influence* on the decision and these can be further distinguished from the *power of decision.*

For each change, the involvement of various individuals and groups in the school is examined by the pressure they have on the change (for or against), by their influence on decisions and the power to decide.

Internal groups are distinguished from external. Internal means that the individuals or groups are involved in that *one* school only and not general educational administration. External means that the individuals or groups are involved in a number of similar social systems or general educational administration. So, for this purpose, parents are classified as internal.*

The whole may be summarised diagrammatically:

Internal	*External*
Teachers, Pupils, Headmaster	Government, H M I, Reports
Housemasters, Chaplain, Prefects, domestic staff	Examinations, Universities
Parents, Governors, Old pupils	Other schools, L E A

Other

Unintended chance events, accidents, etc

* In a later section, however, on the outside world they are seen as mediating agencies between the school and its social and organisational environment (see below pp. 204–5).

2 Decision-making and sources of pressure for and against change

Areas

	Organisation Routine	Social Recreative	Academic	Cultural Creative	Religious Ethical	etc.
(i) INTERNAL						
(ii) EXTERNAL						

For each change: Assess each individual or group for
(a) their pressure for or against change
(b) their influence on the decision
(c) their power to finally decide
Summarise by area for all changes

(i) *INTERNAL*	(ii) *EXTERNAL*
Governors	Government
Headmaster	H M I
Form masters	L E A
Housemasters	Examinations
Heads of Departments	Universities
Staff	Other schools
Bursar	Professional bodies
Caretaker	Subcultural pressures
Chaplain	Neighbourhood pressures
Other staff (domestic, bureaucratic, professional)	Other
Prefects	
Pupils	
Parents	
Ex-pupils	

3 The speed with which change is accomplished

This section analyses the time taken to implement changes in the various areas. The speed with which changes are accomplished involves the time taken to reach a definite decision and the time taken to implement the change once that decision has been made.

Obviously many changes will have been discussed or voted many times in the past but the time to reach a decision implies the time once it has been taken up officially by the decision-making groups.

There are periods in the society's life when change is more likely to occur, for example after the succession of a new headmaster.

3 The speed with which change is accomplished

Area	State time taken to implement change after decision has been made and the time taken to reach a decision for a particular change.	
	Time taken to reach decision	Time taken to implement change
Organisational—routine		
Social—recreative		
Academic		
Cultural—creative		
Religious—ethical		
Administrative		
Athletic		
Pastoral		

4 Effects of changes on roles

We now examine the effects of the changes on the role structure analysed earlier. This should have important bearings for the opposition to changes section. Some structural changes have great impact on the roles of both staff and pupils.

In interviews this section should be fully analysed. For example, a change from a one age group house system to a vertical, all-age house will have profound effects on the roles played by the prefects (pastoral, disciplinary, organisational, to name a few), and often accounts for their conflicts, difficulties and conservative attitudes to change.

5 Mechanisms of achieving change

This section summarises the mechanisms of bringing changes about. The width of the hierarchical span is analysed according to three types: autocratic, oligarchic and democratic. An autocratic process means that the headmaster or headmaster and governors decide alone. Oligarchic implies that the vertical span is still narrow but wider than before (e.g. headmaster, governors and housemasters or senior staff). Democratic means that the span is very wide, covering staff and pupils.

The *process* of decision-making is divided into simple and complex. Simple means that very few sub-bodies are involved, while complex implies that committees or groups of governors, pupils, staff, etc. are brought in to make a complex system of interlocking bodies.

This gives six types of decision-making process, so an autocratic, simple process means that one individual or group decides (e.g. the headmaster) without the involvement of any other bodies in the process of reaching the decision. An autocratic complex process means that the decision is still taken by one or two individuals or groups but the process involves consultation with special-purpose committees and other groups and their representatives.

Although it cannot be represented diagrammatically, data should be collected about the *extent of consultation* in decision-making, Not only is the lateral spread of the consultation important but the depth of consultation in each group.

4 Effects of changes on roles

Instrumental Expressive Organisational

Governors
Headmaster
Housemaster
Heads of Departments
Form masters
etc.

5 Mechanisms of achieving change

	HIERARCHY		
PROCESS	*AUTOCRATIC*	*OLIGARCHIC*	*DEMOCRATIC*
SIMPLE			
COMPLEX			

6 Indices of progress

This section examines what are called the 'indices of progress' held by the school. This is the state of affairs considered satisfactory by the formal order and is a good indication of real goals, judgement on past changes and future trends.

The indices are divided into instrumental, expressive and organisational categories, and in some cases internal and external indices are distinguished.

Obviously, statements such as annual reports or speech day addresses are important here but so are the interview questions on goal achievements and desired qualities of leavers (e.g. headmaster qq.19, 18; housemaster qq.17, 16).

It is useful to compare these indices of progress with the stated goals. The response of the pupil informal social order (the goals they propose) can also be in sharp conflict with the indices, e.g. when the school celebrates a record number of old-boy ordinands while the norms of informal social order are hostile to religion.

We suggested earlier that one index of effectiveness of the institution is the extent and degree of consensus between all interest groups both in their ratings of proposed goals and the extent to which these correlate with their ratings of achieved goals. It is interesting to compare these indices of progress which derive from other sources, with effectiveness as measured by consensus.

6 Indices of progress

INSTRUMENTAL:

Internal Academic: (i) Oxbridge results
                     (ii) 'O'/'A' level results
          Vocational achievements
          Social training
          Citizenship
          Physical fitness, health.

External Ex-pupil academic success
          Ex-pupil social success

EXPRESSIVE:

Internal Sport success, results
          Religious
          Ethical
          Cultural—success
          Personal—character building, forming
          Sportive—spirit, etc.
          Homely

External Prestige in local area

ORGANISATIONAL:

          Continuity over time
          Servicing the organisation
          Control—order, discipline
          Filling time—keeping them occupied
          Money acquired
          Money spent
          Size
          Recruitment—staff, pupils

7 Summary of changes

We provide a useful way of summarising changes that have occurred in a school. The changes are classified in two ways: by the *areas* where they have occurred and according to their *effects* on goals and institutional structure.

The areas concerned are instrumental ones (towards greater or less academic stress), expressive areas (towards greater or less emphasis on expressive values), of organisational areas (the school's aim of self-maintenance). The effects are changes in real goals, changes in institutional structure, or changes which involve no alteration of institutional structure.

This summary table has been found to be a sensitive guide to the degree and areas of changes, and makes possible comparisons between different kinds of school and their patterns of change. It has been possible to construct an index of change in various schools and compare them within this theoretical framework (see Lambert 1969).

Changes that have occurred or changes individuals wish to see are very easily analysed, as they are definite concrete phenomena and so can be dealt with quantitatively and qualitatively.

Information about the changes achieved and those desired is discussed in every interview (headmaster qq.6, 7, 12; housemaster qq.9, 10, 11). For each change, the interview should cover each area of analysis given in this chapter.

Problems arise, however, in the analysis of the pressure groups for and against changes and those involved in the decision-making processes. Interviews are important but the material gathered may be shallow because decision-making processes are so complex and involve many other people.

Documents are very useful for illuminating these problems. Minute books, proceedings of finance and staff meetings, documents sent to parents, internal reports and papers are all useful. (Documents have an importance for many sociological areas. It is too often assumed that documentary evidence is only suitable for basic facts or case records.)

An analysis of all the interview and documentary material from different sources should pinpoint the pressure groups for and against changes, the degree of consultation and any significant role changes which follow. Respondents to questions on change in-

7 Summary of changes

	Instrumental		*Expressive*	*Organisational*
	Towards high academic emphasis	Away from high academic emphasis	Towards expressive emphasis	Away from expressive emphasis

Changes in :

Real goals

Institutional
structure

Non-structural
change

variably indicate the way such changes affect their role sets.

The pupils' replies to questions on changes (q.81), curriculum q.12 and the ' perception of decision-making ' (p. 293) throw light on the pupils' support and desire for change as well as the degree to which they are consulted. Such material offers a useful insight into pupils' interpretation of the power structure of the school which can be compared with the situation discussed in the headmaster's interview (questions 9, 10, 12, 13).

8 Bibliography

The following texts are relevant to the chapter on change:
G. Bernbaum 1967; B. R. Clark 1956; J. C. Dancy 1963; A. G. Frank 1964; R. L. Simpson 1962; J. O. Thompson 1958; I. Weinberg 1967; J. B. Wilson 1962.

VII Authority, status and elites

We have seen how officers in subunits each have a role set. They are accorded power to perform these roles by the formal social order which prescribes the boundaries within which such power can be legitimately exercised. Hence legitimised power can be called authority, 'institutionalised power which is recognised by those over whom the authority is wielded and by the formal social order'. This authority varies according to its amount, the areas over which it is exercised and in the rewards and sanctions which enforce it. Authority is a scarce resource by definition. There will be competition both among the authority holders themselves and between them and any groups who are without it. Individuals may seek to extend their boundaries of influence by using informal power which they hope will be legitimised, such as a senior pupil without authority who corrects the behaviour of a junior.

Not all roles carry authority, however, particularly pupil roles. A fifth former has no greater authority than a first former or third former but he does have higher status in the formal social order and this makes it easier for him to wield informal power over junior pupils. Status, therefore, can be defined as 'the respect and recognition accorded to an individual or a role by others'. A status position in itself may carry visible privileges or symbols, but the status holder cannot offer rewards or exercise sanctions. When recognised by the formal order it can be defined as formal status (e.g. sixth former), where recognised by the informal order it is informal status (e.g. sportsmen). Authority and status are not necessarily concomitant. It is difficult to find an example of a large amount of authority without any status but the reverse, status without authority is possible as in the case of a non-prefect sixth former who wins a scholarship and great status thereby.

Lastly a special kind of a status group is analysed, the elite.

1   Authority

For a topic of such importance this section may seem brief but much that is relevant to it has been included elsewhere. Roles, subunits and change are all relevant to authority. Here we concentrate on the nature of the authority itself.

(i)   Magnitude and distribution of formal authority in areas and subunits The first section examines the magnitude and distribution of formal authority in areas of school life and in subunits, and this gives a picture of the basic authority structure of the school, for example a Public School has a large number of authority holders among staff and pupils. Secondary Modern Schools less for staff and very few for pupils.

(ii)   Nature of authority in schools Section (ii) examines the nature of the authority wielded by each officer. We understand ' nature ' as comprising, first, the *scope* of authority, i.e. the areas of the pupil's life which both formal and informal orders agree authority can invade; secondly, the *roles* played by the authority holders, whether predominantly instrumental, expressive or organisational; and thirdly, the *range* of pupils over whom the authority is wielded.

Such an analysis illustrates the difference between boarding schools and day schools where there is a great difference in the nature of staff authority as well as in the authority structure itself.

Two summaries of the authority system follow. The first examines the degree of delegation of staff duties to pupil authority holders on a simple, elaborate basis. This, in fact, is a summary of a section on pupil roles.

The second relates authority in the school to authority in one of the major subunits—the house—to examine the congruence of authority positions in each system for offices and authority based on age.

1 Authority

(i) Magnitude and distribution of formal authority in areas and subunits

Assess magnitude of authority in area and subunit for:

	Areas	*Subunits*
Staff authority positions	Organisation—Routine	School
Pupil authority positions	Social—Recreative	House
Pupils by *age group*:	Academic	Games
(sixth, fifth, fourth, etc.)	Cultural—Creative	Corps
and for school officers	Religious—Ethical	Religion
house officers	Administrative	Societies
offices in other subunits	Athletic	
	Pastoral	

(ii) Nature of authority in school

For each authority position assess:

(a) the *scope* of authority

Restricted to organisation/routine matters only

Restricted to instrumental and organisational areas only

Universal, personal, private and individual expressive areas

(b) *the nature of the roles played by the authority holders*
(see section on roles)

Instrumental roles

Expressive roles

Organisational roles

(c) *the range* of pupils over whom authority is wielded

Whole school

One subunit of school

One age group (state which)

Most evidence for this section comes from questions on roles in all interviews, special interviews with office holders (see head boy's interview, p. 310) and official lists. Interview evidence and pupils' role sheet results should offer some evidence on the authority roles in the school.

(1) Distributed among a small group of pupils
(2) Distributed among a whole year group

Summary: (iv) Integration of pupil authority in school and house
Assess for (a) Office
          (b) Age group
whether authority in school and house is:
          (1) Separate
          (2) Coincident

2 Status

This section examines the structure of the status system, formal and informal, in the school.

Status may be defined as ' the respect and recognition accorded to an individual or to a role by others '. Formal status will be recognised by symbolic differentiation or privileges, or both, visible to the whole school or smaller units, but it is not necessarily concomitant with authority, for example the scholarship holder previously mentioned or the lower sixth former.

Section (i) examines the areas of school life in which status is accorded in the formal and informal orders. The areas used are the eight areas of school life found in previous sections.

Formal status positions are examined to see if there are any differences in the means of appointing officers in school and house or for roles demanding special aptitudes. The main distinction is between appointment and election as the means of achieving formal status. Many Progressive Schools allocate high status positions by election and their status patterns contrast with schools where staff make the appointments.

Evidence for formal status comes mainly from staff and pupil interviews, though house books and prefect autobiographies often list status positions. Informal status is examined in both pupil interviews and writings (qq.72, 74, 75, 76, 77, 78).

The orientation of informal status groups must always be examined for they may work against the goals of the school (e.g. bullies, pupils who are anti-games, anti-culture) though in some schools the informal status groups are supportive of these goals (e.g. games heroes, intellectuals) and the formal and informal status systems may be highly congruent.

The presence of formal and informal status groups is closely related to the relative strengths of the formal and informal social orders and the relationship between them. This was analysed in detail in an earlier section (p. 129).

2 Status

(i) *Status holders*
List all those with formal and informal status and classify for the
eight areas in which their status lies.

(ii) *Means of achieving formal status*
    Examine for each officer:

Appointment	*Election*
(a) By merit	(a) By whole school
(b) By seniority	(b) By limited section of school
(c) Other	(c) By group of status holders

Examine *the means of achievement* to house, to school offices and
to expressive and organisational positions.

	Appointment	*Appointment and Election*	*Election*
House Officers			
School Officers			
Organisational Officers			
Expressive Officers			

Informal status
Summarise activities which confer high informal status. Classify
these activities and examine whether they are oriented towards or
from (i) school's stated goals and (ii) the norms of the informal
order.

Instrumental

                Academic
                Vocational
                Social training
                Citizenship
                Physical

Expressive

                Religious
                Ethical
                Cultural
                Personal development
                Self discipline
                Homely

3 Elites: The nature of formal and informal elites

Certain formal and informal status groups (not individuals) may be an *elite*. The concept ' status ' examined prestige from the point of view of the whole society. That of the ' elites ' analyses the situation from a different angle, by membership i.e. from the elite's point of view. In other words, informal elites represent an analysis of the formal organisation of informal groups.

The term ' elite ' means a high status group (formal or informal) which is self-selecting and self-perpetuating. Probably the most famous example is Pop at Eton, though many schools have intellectual, games or social elites within their sixth form, or within various year-groupings.

Section (i) examines the areas of school life where formal and informal elites arise.

Section (ii) relates the multiplicity or number of elites to their exclusiveness and degree of separate identity. In some schools many loosely formed elites compete with one another whilst in other schools there is just one very exclusive formal or informal elite.

In section (iii) the elites are examined for their orientation to goals and norms. This is especially important for informal elites, as often they have a profound influence on the informal social order and play some part in determining informal norms.* In schools where there is one exclusive informal elite, this elite can be a strong informal power group oriented towards or away from goals.

Evidence for this section comes from the same source as status, though sociometric tests can often confirm other evidence, as can the friendship group question to pupils (q.71).

---

* The factors determining the origins of informal norms are obscure. Our research has shown that in boarding schools it is quite false to assume that they are a *direct* response to single factors (e.g. totality, reference groups of pupils) because schools with very similar structures show very different norms. It is likely that different norms have different causes. Among the causes more relevant possibly are previous social and educational backgrounds of staff and pupils, cyclical fashions of behaviour, the institutionalised culture of each school and subunits into which new pupils are socialised, and the values and styles embraced by the elites. Much fruitful sociological research could be done on this topic.

3 Elites: The nature of formal and informal elites

(i) *AREAS WHERE THEY ARISE*

Organisation—Routine
Social-Recreative
Academic
Cultural—Creative
Religious—Ethical
Administrative
Athletic
Pastoral

(ii) *MULTIPLICATION OF ELITES*

	Number of elites	
One single elite	A few major elites e.g. 2-4	Many competing elites
(1) Each elite has a separate identity and is exclusive to other elites	Examine for formal and informal elites	
(2) Membership of elites overlaps		

(iii) *ORIENTATION OF ELITES*

Examine orientation of formal and informal elites to:

GOALS Instrumental:

Examine for orientation to:
(a) Stated goals
(b) Norms of informal order

Expressive:
Norms:

4 Summaries

Two summaries follow to try to relate all these interlinked concepts.

(i) Correspondence of formal authority, informal status and informal power Section (i) links formal authority with informal status and informal power. Informal power was partly dealt with in the sections on *change, on influences on change* (p. 170). If a comparison is made between this informal power and the first section of this chapter (p. 182) on the magnitude and distribution of authority and the section on informal status (p. 186) the three may not correspond. The comparison below clarifies the areas and offices where such discrepancies occur.

	Formal Authority	*Informal Status among pupils*	*Status among staff*	*Informal Power*
Disciplinarian housemaster	High	Low	High	High
Leading figure in pupil underlife	Low	High	Low	High
Bully	Low	Low	Low	High

(ii) Balance between organisational roles, authority and privilege in pupil officers We now examine the extent to which the status bearers commit themselves to the goals of the school. This depends on the relationship between duties assigned to them, the authority they wield, and the privileges they receive. A simple framework is constructed, based on the acceptance of organisational roles, authority and privilege by the pupils' informal social order. As the pupil social order evaluates them as adequate or inadequate, so we have eight different patterns. Some patterns make for effective working of the authority system while others make for alienation of the office holders or tyranny.

Information for this summary comes from lists of offices, interviews with officers (especially prefects) and staff (housemaster qq.3, 6), senior boys' autobiographies are also a good guide to status positions at various ages and the problems associated with them.

4 Summaries

(i) Correspondence of formal authority, informal status and informal power among staff and school officers

	Eight Areas	
	Organisation—Routine Social—Recreative etc.	
	FORMAL	INFORMAL	INFORMAL
	AUTHORITY	STATUS	POWER

List: Staff Offices
      Pupil Offices
      Pupil Elites

(ii) Balance between organisational roles, authority and privilege in pupil officers

Organisational Roles	Authority	Privilege	Effect
x	x	x	Effective working
x	y	x	Effective but occasional abuse of
y	x	x	power
x	x	y	Frustration and disaffection
y	y	x	
x	y	y	
y	y	y	Alienation of office holders with
y	x	y	likelihood of tyranny or abuse

x = amount is defined as adequate by the pupil informal social order
y = amount is defined as too much (in the case of organisational roles) or too little (in the case of authority or privilege)

Until now our consideration of the goals and the mechanisms of achieving them has concentrated on the constituent parts of the social system of the school. However the achievement of many goals also depends on influences exerted by other social systems which impinge on the school and it is these wider aspects which we consider next.

5 Bibliography

The following texts are relevant to the chapter on authority, status and elites:
Authority:
H. S. Becker 1953; R. Dahrendorf 1959; A. Etzioni 1962; N. Gross 1965; W. Waller 1932; C. Washbourne 1957; R. Wilkinson 1964.
Status and Elites:
W. A. L. Blyth 1958; T. B. Bottomore 1964; D. S. Cartwright 1961; J. S. Coleman 1961; C. W. Gordon 1957; A. W. Halpin 1956; A. N. Oppenheim 1955; M. Seeman 1960; C. Shrag 1954; R. L. Simpson 1952; R. Wilkinson 1964.

VIII The school in the wider social setting

The framework so far has concentrated on the school as a system in itself, its structure, operation, the forces making for integration or conflict between the various parts.

Nevertheless, it is important to remember that schools exist along with other social systems, parasystems, which to some extent determine the nature of the system of the school. The school cannot be isolated from the wider social system, as changes in this wider one will be a pressure for changes in the social system of the school.

This chapter therefore examines the relationship between the school and its parasystems.

These are discussed according to the following areas:
1 Recruitment to the school
2 Social background of teachers, governors, parents and pupils
3 School's relations with parents
4 School activities and outside agencies
5 Individual activities and outside agencies
6 The local neighbourhood
7 Relations with other schools

Finally it presents a sociological typology of the various functioning subunits in the school and the outside or mediating bodies which impinge upon them, and then a discussion and model of the relationship between these pressures and the functions or dysfunctions for the society which result from them.

1   Recruitment to the school

One factor which will impinge on the school social system is the pattern of recruitment—both the reasons for parents sending their children and the selectivity of the admission process. This short section examines the parental reasons for sending pupils to the school and the selectivity involved. The headmaster's interview, pupil questionnaire qq.32, 38, 39 and 49, and parents' interviews provide all the necessary information.

2   The social background of staff, governors, parents and pupils

Recent studies have stressed the importance of the social background of administrators, staff, parents and pupils as a factor which exerts a strong influence on the acceptance of many school goals. The areas discussed are the educational background of staff, governors, parents and pupils. The immediate educational background of the pupils is important, as some pupils have been consciously prepared for a certain school. Observers have noted how the Grammar School ethos is inculcated in the top streams of Primary Schools.

Section 2 outlines the social class of these groups. Occupations can be classified according to the Registrar General's Classification of Occupations. In the case of pupils it is important to consider the class of two reference groups (a reference group is a group by which an individual evaluates himself); first that of the pupils' contemporaries and secondly that of their future occupational groups. These reference groups are important, since the strong influence of 'mass youth culture' does not prevent considerable differences in culture between schools or differential stress on certain aspects of 'mass youth culture' within any one school.

The subsequent sections deal with the income of parents, with religion, with political sympathies. The region of origin may be important because if staff and parents have local ties to the area and school or if they are basically immigrant their response to the school may differ. This section is followed by an examination of the accessibility of the school as long distances for pupils to travel and fixed bus timetables can influence much of the extracurricular activities of schools and the social life of the pupils.

1 Recruitment to the school

(i) No effective parental choice of school—no or little selection

(ii) Parental choice for types of school —entry selective
—little or no selection

(iii) Parental necessity for this kind of—entry selective
school (e.g. vocational, special or—little or no selection
residential school)

(iv) Necessity for this kind of school but—entry selective
recruitment administered by L E A or—little or no selection
other body

2 The social background of staff, governors, parents and pupils

Give relevant details for each:
Educational background
Social class
Income
Political sympathies
Region of origin
Marital status
Proximity of residence

3 The school's relations with parents

Section 3 examines the nature of the school's relations with parents and, for residential schools, the amount of parental contact allowed at home and school.

4 School activities and outside agencies

This section examines the relationship between *school* activities and outside agencies, the outside events or organisations to which children go in school parties and, secondly, visits to the school by outside groups.

3 The school's relations with parents

State frequency:
  (i)   Encourages parents to come to the school to *participate* in things
 (ii)   Encourages parents to come to the school as an *audience*
(iii)   Lays on talks or events specifically for parents *as a body*
 (iv)   Parents form themselves into a distant, organised body
  (v)   Parents lay on activities for school to participate in, dances, talks, etc.
 (vi)   Individual parents encouraged to come with problems about children

Relations between parents and children (residential schools only)

  (i)   Details of restrictions about children seeing their parents
        Frequency of maximum permitted contact
        Frequency of average contact
 (ii)   Details of restrictions about children going home
        Frequency of maximum permitted contact
        Frequency of average number of visits

4 School activities and outside agencies

  (i)   *Outside events or organisations to which children go in school parties*
        Give events for last term:
        Type: *Junior   Middle   Senior* pupils
            Academic
            Vocational
            Cultural
            Sportive
            Recreative
            Social
            Religious
            Citizenship

5 Individual activities and outside agencies

This section examines the events or organisations children go to *individually* in their free time. The same framework is used as for section 4 but a wider range of pupil ages is given.

Finally, more details must be recorded of leisure pursuits even if they are subject to the pressures of changing fashions.

(ii) *Visits to the school*   Number/Term
     Type:
          Academic
          Vocational
          Cultural
          Sportive
          Recreative
          Social
          Religious
          Citizenship

5 Individual activities and outside agencies

Events or organisation children go to individually in their own free time:
     Type: *Junior   Middle   Senior* pupils
                                              Boys—Girls
          Academic
          Vocational
          Cultural
          Sportive
          Recreative
          Social
          Religious
          Citizenship
     Specify details of:
          Youth Clubs
          Church organisations
          Scouts/Guides
          Political parties
          Supporters Clubs

6 The local neighbourhood

Section 6 deals with the nature of the local neighbourhood and its relationship with the school.

The predominant social class of the neighbourhood should be compared with the class of the pupils attending the school. Obviously it is difficult to fit a meaningful generalisation into a general typology. Perhaps some indices like Juror index, rateable values, level of home ownership, etc. may be a lead.

The predominant industry is also a vague category, but the nature of local employment, the proportion of working mothers and the juvenile unemployment rate may be important influences on the aspirations and leaving patterns of the pupils.

Thirdly, a general comparison is made between the class background and residential experience of pupils and the local area. Some special schools are in a neighbourhood quite unlike the home areas of their pupils.

The last section examines the school's relationship with the neighbourhood in two ways, the school in the neighbourhood and the neighbourhood in the school.

6 The local neighbourhood

(i) *Predominant social class of neighbourhood around school*
Professional
Middle class
Lower middle/upper working class
Working class

(ii) *Predominant industry in local area*
Predominant employment and industries
% of women in population employed
% of unemployed juveniles

(iii) *Neighbourhood and children's backgrounds*
Examine the congruence between the class and nature of the neighbourhood of the school and the background of the pupils for:

	High	Low
Class background		
Residential background (e.g. urban/rural)		

(iv) *School's relationship with the neighbourhood*
(a) *School in neighbourhood*

	Frequency
Participates actively in local activities, societies, politics, etc.	
Supports, goes as an audience, church, theatre	
Ignores local neighbourhood	

(b) *Neighbourhood in school*

Certain local officials (e.g. vicars) take part in school life	
Local people join in school's activities, societies	
Invites and encourages local people to come as an audience	
Locality use school buildings for evening classes, meetings etc.	
Ignores local neighbourhood	

7 Relations with other schools

Lastly in this section, the relationship between the school and other schools is examined.

Details for all this section on neighbourhood must come during interviews, examination of society minutes and questioning often over meals or semi-formal occasions, as it is a respectable yet important topic for conversation.

7 Relations with other schools

(i) *SINGLE-SEX SCHOOLS*

(a) *OF SAME SEX ONLY*:

NUMBER/TERM

	Same type of school	Different type of school
Sport		
Plays, concerts		
Societies		

(b) *OF OTHER SEX*:

	Same type of school	Different type of school
Sport		
Plays, concerts		
Societies		
Dances		

(ii) *MIXED SCHOOLS*:

	Same type of school	Different type of school
Sport		
Plays, concerts		
Societies		
Dances		

8 The school and other organisations

In the framework opposite, we analyse the school's relationship with the organisations it meets at its own boundaries.

Such organisations may be *mediating organisations* in that they stand between the school and yet other organisations; such mediating organisations might be Governors, Parents Organisations, Old Pupils' Associations, feeding schools, and, to a lesser extent, the L E A. The other organisations are still more *external* to the school, though their externality varies from that of an Exam Board or the Ministry in London, to the firm which services the duplicator or does the catering.

While the school performs its basic instrumental and expressive functions, relatively few external organisations impinge *directly* on it, or penetrate it as an organisation, or render it organisationally *dependent* on them. (*Indirectly*, however, such external bodies may be critically important—e.g. university entrance requirements may dictate the form and content of teaching.)

In performing its organisational functions, however, the situation is different. For the purposes of this section we have subdivided organisational functions into (a) *managerial*, those concerned with tasks of direction, adjudication and control; (b) *maintenance functions*, those which enable a proper performance of institutional roles; (c) *adaptive functions*: enabling the school to change; (d) *supportive functions*: enabling the school to recruit or dispose of members and conduct relations with outside bodies. Under each heading we denote subunits which function (in whole or part) in each way.

On the right-hand side are the mediating or external organisations which impinge on them. It will be seen that it is in these organisational areas that most outside organisations impinge directly on the school, and chiefly in the areas of maintenance and adaptations. Supportive functions are performed largely by mediating organisations.

8 The school and other organisations

  (i) *Instrumental and expressive functions*

Subunits	Outside organisations impinging
Academic	Universities, Examination Boards, Inspectorate, Parents
Athletic	Other schools
Religious	

  (ii) *Organisational functions*

(a) *Managerial functions of direction, adjudication and control*

Subunits	Outside organisations impinging
Authority	Governors (L E A)
Control	

(b) *Maintenance functions: enabling the proper performance of institutional roles*

Subunits	Outside organisations impinging
Pastoral, counselling	Parents, Youth Service
Domestic	
Secretarial	Commercial organisations
	Trade Unions
	Government
	Inspectorate
Sanatorium	

(c) *Adaptive functions: enabling the school to change*

Subunits	Outside organisations impinging
Communications	Other schools
Public relations	L E AS and Central Departments
	H M I
	Universities, Colleges, Examination Boards
	Employers
	Parents

(d) *Supportive functions: enabling the organisation to recruit, or dispose of members or conduct outside relations*

	Outside organisations impinging
(1) *recruitment*	feeding schools
subsystem:	L E AS
junior department	Governors

9 Effects of direct penetration by outside organisations

Finally, opposite we present a diagram of the degree of penetration by outside or mediating bodies which are functional or dysfunctional for the society, in terms of attaining its goals.

A high degree of external penetration is functional for the supportive, adaptive and maintenance areas, but those schools which possess more or less impenetrable boundaries, may generate severe dysfunctions, which prevent change and adequate operation. For example, schools without close relations with employers or the youth employment service or universities may inadequately place their leavers (disposal functions), those with minimal relations with parents and other bodies may engender an unsatisfactory reputation (public relations functions).

On the other hand, high direct penetration may be severely dysfunctional for managerial and the major instrumental and expressive functions and obstruct these basic processes. For example, an interfering L E A can obstruct the decision-making process in the school, and examining boards can induce frequent changes of curriculum which impair the teaching function of the school.

Indirect penetration may or may not be dysfunctional.

This chapter has been empirical but nevertheless is very important. It is the sort of area in which research must be guided by some overall programme theory or hypothesis, as unlimited material can otherwise be gathered. All this manual can offer is some general concepts, such as the presenting culture, and some indices by which it can be assessed.

Basic data about the background of staff and pupils comes from interviews (headmaster q.1; housemaster q.1; head of school q.1), pupil replies to qq.20-26, 31-39 and the parents' interview schedule

(2) *disposal*	Governors
	Employers (Youth Employment Services, Universities, Colleges, Examination Boards)
(3) *public relations*	Parents
	Old Boys
	Governors

9 Effects of direct penetration by outside organisations

	Functional Situations	*Dysfunctional Situations*
High penetration by outside organisations	Supportive and adaptive functions Maintenance functions	Managerial functions Expressive functions
Low penetration by outside organisations	Managerial functions Instrumental and expressive functions	Maintenance functions Adaptive and Supportive functions

(High penetration may be functional or otherwise for instrumental functions.)

(p. 315). Data from all these sources make it possible to investigate the impact of outside cultural forces on the school.

The relationship of the school to the neighbourhood and other schools can be assessed from details in the scale in institutional control (p. 317) and pupils' contact with the local neighbourhood (qq.50-52). Parental and home contact is covered in the parents' questionnaire and pupil question 50.

The activities to which children go out of school and the impact of the local community are best followed by participant observation and discussion with groups of staff and pupils. Documents and magazines are also useful as they list fixtures and outings.

10   Bibliography

The following texts are relevant to the chapter on the school in the wider social setting:

B. Berger 1963; W. A. L. Blyth 1965; M. Castle 1954; J. S. Coleman 1960, 1961; L. Davison; J. W. B. Douglas 1964; C. E. Fishbourne 1962; J. Floud 1962; R. Giallombardo 1966; D. H. Hargreaves 1967; A. B. Hollingshead 1962; B. Jackson 1962; G. Kalton 1966; P. Masters 1966; W. G. Mollenkopf F. Musgrove 1961; K. Ollerenshaw 1967; T. Parsons 1954; K. Pringle 1957; C. W. Sherif 1964; E. A. Smith 1962; S. Soles 1964; B. Sugarman 1967.

IX The effectiveness of the organisation

The final chapter of this framework examines the effectiveness of the organisation. Most of the previous chapters have examined the factors making for effectiveness but the definition of effectiveness has always been narrow and concerned with the achievement of the goals which the school sets itself. It is within these conceptual limits that all the previous chapters are relevant. However there are two wider dimensions in which effectiveness can be judged: (1) in terms of achieving the expectations and demands of the school's parasystems and (2) in terms of the school's functions for the wider society.

Effectiveness, therefore, can be examined in three ways:

1 Effectiveness in achieving goals
2 Effectiveness in achieving the expectations and demands of the school's parasystems
3 Effectiveness in fulfilling functions for the wider society.

While this book has explored the first of these, the other two kinds should not be ignored because, though a school may achieve its own goals (e.g. religious or pastoral), it may fail to meet the demands of a particular parasystem (e.g. local employers who want technicians). Further to this, the school, whatever its goals, may have the function for the wider society of promoting social mobility or the maintenance of social stratification. However aspirant the goals of a working class, non-selective school may be, considerable research has shown that in such schools the number of children who achieve social mobility by the educational process remains very small. Hence one of the school's latent functions is to maintain patterns of social stratification. The same is true of Public Schools which despite the stress of egalitarian goals such as service and consideration for others cannot escape their function of fashioning an elite in society. Nowhere is this particular difference more marked than in independent Quaker Schools, where there is an open conflict between egalitarian ethos and elitist function.

First, then, we look at effectiveness in terms of achieving goals, as it is with this area that the manual is most concerned.

1 Effectiveness in achieving goals

The first framework, which covers two pages, examines the indices by which the school's effectiveness in achieving goals can be judged. The areas considered are related to the previous chapters of the framework. They are: goals, communications, control, relationship between the formal and informal social orders, roles, change and parasystems. Each area is a subdivision of the factors which promote effectiveness in achieving goals, since so many of these factors are mutually interdependent. It should be noted that these indices are set in both a functional and a conflict context, for not all conflicts make for effectiveness, as we have seen of certain goal conflicts and conflicts in individual role sets. Some conflicts, however, do make for a structural conduciveness to change and contribute to the effectiveness of the organisation.

Each of the seven indices is measured by *objective* means, from standard tests, and in many cases it is possible to create numerical indices of effectiveness, as is done by the social adaptation test, that for goals or the content of norms. Hence subjective assessment is avoided.

One further problem remains, however. The indices are often arranged on dimensions 'high—low, congruent—incompatible'. Obviously, it is difficult to judge where 'high' begins and 'low' ends, even in those indices which are numerical. Clearly for some indices there are optimum or critical divides at which effective consequences become ineffective. Attempts to assess where the critical divides are will be made in the main report of this research project but it will suffice in this document to suggest that this is an area where further research will add to what has gone before.

It should be remembered that some aspects of the effectiveness of the organisation may not be desirable educationally or socially. Many critics of Public and Progressive Schools, for example, have suggested that the ethos is too effectively imbibed by some pupils who become dependent on the school for support and security and so may fail to adjust in later life.

1 Effectiveness in achieving goals

GOALS *Instrumental*: Academic, vocational, social training, citizenship, physical development
Expressive: Religious, ethical, cultural, personal development, sportsmanship, homely
Organisational: Continuity over time, servicing organisation, control, filling in time, maintaining reputation

	EFFECTIVE	*Means of Assessment*	INEFFECTIVE
GOALS':			
(i)	Academic results consistent with ability of pupils	Records of results, pupil ability, intelligence	Academic results inconsistent with ability of pupils
(ii)	High consensus between staff, parents' and pupils' ratings of proposed and achieved goals	Goal sheet, q.1, q.86. Interviews	Low consensus between staff, parents' and pupils' ratings of proposed and achieved goals
(iii)	High conformity among pupils and staff in areas associated with real goals of school	Merton adaptation test, q.82, q.85, q.87.	Low conformity among pupils and staff in areas associated with real goals of school
(iv)	Balance between instrumental, expressive and organisational goals or conflict situations where instrumental and expressive goals dominate organisational or where instrumental and organisational dominate expressive goals.	Goal summary	Goal conflict situations where organisational goals dominate instrumental and expressive goals, where expressive goals dominate instrumental and organisational goals
COMMUNICATION:	Congruence between types of communication between subunits and age ranges and goal areas	Interviews. Perception of decision-making	Incompatibility between types of communication between subunits and age ranges and goal areas
CONTROL:	Congruence between methods of social control and goal areas	Interviews	Incompatibility between methods of social control and goal areas

RELATIONSHIP BETWEEN FORMAL AND INFORMAL SOCIAL ORDERS:		
(i) Congruence of formal and informal norms	Orientation of norms q.89, q.74, q.75, q.76, q.77, q.85	Incompatibility of formal and informal norms
(ii) Congruence of formal and informal social orders in areas of status, elites	q.72, q.73, q.74, q.75, q.76, q.77, q.85	Incompatibility between formal and informal orders in areas of status and elites
(iii) Close staff-pupil relations	Staff-pupil relations test Pastoral Care q.65, q.66, q.67	Distant staff-pupil relations
ROLES:		
(i) Congruence of formal role prescriptions and informal evaluation of roles	Role sheet. Interviews	Incompatibility between formal role prescriptions and informal evaluation of roles
(ii) Low degree of *structural* role conflicts, high or low conflict in individual role sets		High degree of *structural* role conflicts, high or low conflict in individual role sets
CHANGE:		
Structural conduciveness for change to meet new pressures	Interview with headmaster q.84	Structure unable to adapt to meet new pressures
PARASYSTEMS:		
(i) Congruence between expectations of leavers (as related to parents' social class) and actual destination	Interviews	Incompatibility between expectations of leavers (as related to parents' social class) and actual destinations
(ii) High penetration by parasystems in supportive, adaptive and maintenance areas, low penetration in managerial, instrumental and expressive areas.		High penetration by parasystems in managerial and expressive areas, low penetration in maintenance, adaptive and supportive areas.

2   Effectiveness and parasystems

The next section examines the effectiveness of the school in achieving the expectations and demands of the various parasystems. A particular parasystem, e.g. an employer, may only be interested in the achievement of certain goals (e.g. academic, social training) and may be unconcerned with other goals (e.g. religious, ethical). Hence the school may be effective in terms of the parasystem's narrow expectations but ineffective in terms of its total system of real goals.

3   Effectiveness and functions for the wider society

We turn now from the school's immediate parasystems to a larger context. We look at the functions which the school has for the wider society. As we saw earlier, they fall into three kinds: allocative, integrative and administrative.

The school may be effective in fulfilling some of these functions whether or not it achieves its own real goals or the goals proposed by parasystems. A leading Public School and a Secondary Modern School may both function according to 1a, 2c, 3a, b, c, opposite, though one may be more effective in achieving its own goals than the other.

2 Effectiveness and parasystems

REAL GOALS OF SCHOOL	*GOALS PROPOSED BY PARASYSTEMS*	
Instrumental	Instrumental	Parents
Expressive	Expressive	Employers
Organisational	Organisational	Universities
		Examination Board
		L E A
		Old Pupils
		Governors

3 Effectiveness and functions for the wider society

(i) *Allocative functions*
  (a) Agent for maintaining patterns of social stratification
  (b) Agent of social mobility

(ii) *Integrative functions*
  (a) Providing education
  (b) Socialising, transmitting values, culture, norms
  (c) Agents for delineating children's or adolescent roles
  (d) Agent for training in adult roles

(iii) *Administrative functions*
  (a) Agent of social and medical welfare
  (b) Custodial functions, keeping children together under control
  (c) Replacing family as agent in charge of children for short periods of time

X The sociology of the classroom unit

So far in this manual we have considered the school in general. We now bring the main perspectives and methods used in this general analysis to bear on one basic situation which is found in all schools, however much they differ in other respects: the teacher and a group of pupils interacting in the classroom. It will be seen that the basic sociological approaches, suitably modified, enable an understanding of the nature, effectiveness and dynamics of this fundamental unit of the school. Much of the methodology is also relevant. But for the study of the school class, there is no substitute for persistent observation over time, using systematic recording methods and subsequent classification of data.

1 Outside determinants

What goes on in the classroom and its effectiveness as a means of transmission, is conditioned, sometimes absolutely, by the whole aims, structure and operation of the school. Of particular importance are, however, these features of the organisation, as a whole.

(i) *Goals*: If the school has a high instrumental stress, say on exams, then classes of non-exam subjects (e.g. general science or art) may be adversely affected. Conversely, if the school stresses some expressive ends, let us say creativity, some classes concerned with instrumental goals (e.g. P.E. or games) may be adversely affected. Similarly, the degree of organisational stress in the school may limit the flexibility of the class: for example, in a school where discipline is highly emphasised it may be difficult to adopt certain modes of classroom presentation most suited to the subject.

(ii) *Roles*: The role system among staff and pupils defines the nature of their interaction and may be difficult to modify in the individual classroom setting.

(iii) *Control*: The system of control used in the school again may affect the effectiveness of the class, so that, if the school uses predominantly coercive or normative methods, it may be difficult for the teacher to modify these and this inability may affect his relationship with the class.

(iv) *Norms*: The norms and nature of staff-pupil relations in general can hinder or help the teacher's task with the particular class.

(v) *Informal order*: The whole nature of the pupil informal order conditions the teacher's effectiveness and the pupil's response to the teaching situation. Pupil norms, the informal system of status and elites among them, their patterns of association in general may influence the reactions of any one group of pupils in the classroom situation.

So much for the general determinants of the classroom situation. What sociological areas of analysis apply within its walls, what are the structure and dynamics of the situation of a teacher actually taking a forty-minute lesson? What elements of an organisational approach can be applied to this fundamental situation in the school, this miniature society within a society?

1   Outside determinants

(i) *Nature of school goals*: Degree of stress on instrumental expressive, organisational ends, affects reception of subject matter and mode of presentation.

(ii) *Role system of school*: Defines structure of teacher-pupil interaction in classroom unit.

(iii) *The system of control*: In the school affects that used in the class and the degree to which it can be modified.

(iv) *The norms and nature of staff-pupil relations*: In general condition the specific relationship of the class to the teacher.

(v) *The informal society of the pupils*: In general affects the structure and dynamics of the society of the class.

2 Content and approach of the lesson

To what degree does the teacher's material and approach exemplify instrumental, expressive or organisational orientation? Is the substance and method concerned with imparting information, developing skills or with transmitting values, developing the self, or all of these and in what proportion? Even between teachers and subjects the stress may differ radically. To what degree do organisational ends predominate: e.g. does the teacher expect strict discipline, silence, order and routine from the class at one extreme, or, at the other, does the class function as loosely informal groupings, moving around, making noise, making diverse demands on the teacher? The more expressive the content, the less organisational methods will be congruent—more congruent would be informal discussion and interchange, and so on.

The pupils' own view on the content and purpose of the particular lesson is vital: do they see it as primarily instrumental (e.g. to get exam results or as a means to a job), or expressive (to develop themselves or grapple with values), or organisational (as a means of killing time, keeping them busy)?

Disparities of view between teachers and class, lack of consensus among the class, incompatibilities between the material and purpose of the lesson and its mode of presentation, help to determine the effectiveness or otherwise, of the lesson as a vehicle of transmission.

The methods of studying this consist of detailed and systematic recording in the classroom situation, interviews with teachers, standard tests with the pupils, e.g. questions on teaching and curriculum, qq.12, 13 in the pupil questionnaire as well as individual items on goals sheet, q.1 and the 'promotes question', q.86.

2   Content and approach of the lesson

The degree to which material and presentation is instrumental, expressive and organisational in orientation.

The degree to which pupils perceive and approve this instrumental, expressive, organisational stress.

Incompatibilities (e.g. expressive ends and organisational methods), disparities (e.g. between teachers' orientation and those of pupils) condition effectiveness.

3 Roles in the classroom

To what degree are the roles played by the teachers and the pupils *already* defined by the structure and operation of the school: what instrumental, expressive and organisational elements are expected to be emphasised in the teacher's classroom role (see above, p. 149) what elements of the pupils' roles (see above, p. 159) are expected to be emphasised? In the actual situation, however, between pupils and teachers, different roles may be performed from those presented and expected. When taking his or her own form in the role of subject teacher, the form master may interpret his role (more relaxed, more intimate) differently from that which he may take up with other forms. When taking a small group of able sixth formers, roles on both sides are likely to be different from those performed in a large class of less able fifth formers. This has major implications for the effectiveness or otherwise of the interaction. The relevant methods are extensive interviewing to establish staff/pupil roles in school, detailed and systematic recording in the classroom situation.

3 Roles in the classroom

Role pattern of teachers—prescribed externally
Role pattern of pupils—prescribed variably

4   Control in the classroom

This is one of the major influences upon effectiveness of transmission in the classroom setting. The teachers may use positive or negative controls or both, those formally laid down or those informally resorted to by himself, though the distinction between formal and informal controls may be blurred in the practice of different schools.

(i) *Positive Controls*: Fall into two kinds, utilitarian and normative.

(a) *Utilitarian controls*: Involve the use of rewards with some material basis, such as marks and reports, prizes, privileges, reducing work or prep or stressing examination results or career benefits. Informal controls of this kind might include relaxing routine (a breather in the classroom time) or offering inducements such as stories at the end of lessons, a film next lesson.

(b) *Normative controls*: Consist of the use of status or consensus among the group; among the most common methods will be public and private praise, promotion or raising formal status, devices to encourage competition among the pupils, the evocation of group approval or parental approval, appealing to the reputation of the individual, the group or the school, stress on an individual's standing or the group's standing in relation to others. Informal methods would include use of Christian names or a style of idiom of approach which identifies with that of the pupils' own society, such as trendy illustrations, possibly risqué jokes, use of 'friends' within the class to influence others, manipulation of the status holders in the pupils' own world in this class.

(ii) *Negative Controls*: Fall into three kinds, coercive, utilitarian and normative.

(a) *Coercive controls*: Have a physical component. Formally they may be limited to caning or strapping, or removing the child from the class altogether. Informally they consist of striking, shaking or throwing or threatening force or expulsion.

(b) *Utilitarian controls*: Consist of deprivations with some material basis, such as poor marks or reports, the removal of material privileges, the imposition of extra work, restrictions on freedom, food, environment (detentions, etc.) the threat of poor exam results, poor career prospects. Informally utilitarian controls are limited, perhaps the most crucial could be removal of

4 Control in the classroom

(i) *POSITIVE*

Utilitarian   —Formal and informal
Normative   —Formal and informal

(ii) *NEGATIVE*

Coercive   —Formal and informal
Utilitarian   —Formal and informal
Normative   —Formal and informal

individuals from radiators, windows, the back of the class, seizure of comics.

(c) *Normative controls*: Involve the use of status or group consensus. Prominent among them will be public or private censure, degradation by lowering formal position or by encouraging disapproval by the group or by parents, using the reputation of the individual, group or school, by arousing feelings of shame or guilt. Informally, negative control may be attempted by use of nicknames, surnames, by verbal controls such as sarcasm, mockery, type-grouping or by shows of coldness, ostracism or rejection.

The balance between types of control differs from school to school and class to class, lesson to lesson. In many schools more or less consistent patterns of control will emerge between positive and negative stress on the one hand and between coercive and normative kinds on the other. Certain hypotheses may be confirmed:
(a) High effectiveness of transmission is attained where positive controls predominate.
(b) The higher the expressive purpose and content of the interaction, the higher the normative control and the lower the coercive kind of control must be for effective transmission.
(c) The higher the organisational element in the method and purpose of the interaction, the higher will be the use of utilitarian and coercive controls.
Data on control systems can be gathered from attitudinal and norms tests from staff and pupils, but essentially from systematically observing, recording each interchange in the classroom situation and classifying afterwards.

(iii) *RELATIONSHIPS BETWEEN CONTROLS AND GOALS*
High effectiveness is related to positive control
Expressive orientation is incompatible with coercive control
Organisational orientation demands greater utilitarian and coercive control

5   The pupils' informal order

The pupils' informal order in the class profoundly influences responses to the content and method of the lesson, the definitions of role and the response to controls. Among the most important elements in the class are: (i) *Patterns of association*: How the pupils are physically grouped and the interactions between and within such groupings. (ii) *How high and low status is distributed*: Among the pupils in the class, which persons exercise leadership roles and which groups possess elite status? The interaction between such persons and groups and the teacher will be a vital factor in the effectiveness of communication and control. (iii) *The pupils' own modes of controlling each other* (see above, p. 112 for the main kinds of control). Awareness and manipulation and direction of these is important for the teacher's own control. (iv) *Informal norms among the pupils* with regard to the subject in question, the degree of work and enthusiasm permitted, the nature of staff-pupil relations.

Data on these aspects can be obtained by standard tests, sociometric tests of the class, observation and recording of the interactions between each member of the class.

5 The pupils' informal order

(i) Patterns of association
(ii) Status, leadership and elite distribution
(iii) Pupils' own system of control
(iv) Informal norms
All affect pupils' response and teacher's control and effectiveness

6 The pupil's adaptations in the class

These can be classified along the general dimension provided earlier in this book (above, p. 122) but modified to suit the specific situation of the class. The basic adaptations will range thus:

(i) *conformity*: Consisting of high commitment to the subject matter, high responsiveness to presentation, high effort, low disturbance.

(ii) *ritualism*: Consisting of low commitment to the subject matter, moderate responsiveness to presentation, moderate effort, low disturbance.

(iii) *retreatism*: Consisting of low commitment to subject, low responsiveness to presentation, low effort and low disturbance (daydreaming, passivity are manifestations, or absenteeism or missing the class).

(iv) *rebellion*: Consisting of low commitment to subject, either low or overdisruptive responsiveness to presentation, low effort and high disturbance.

By periodic testing accompanied by vigilant observation and recording and examination of written work and rough books, it is possible to plot each individual's responses in repeated or different classroom situations. From this, the response of the class as a whole can be ascertained and of the different elements within it. Once this is done, causative factors—nature of subject and presentation, pupil norms, teacher's controls, the dynamics of the pupils' groupings and leadership patterns—can be examined and interrelationships established. Thus it is possible to hypothesise the likely relationships between the teachers' predominant kind of control and predominant responses by the pupils.

(i) *Where coercive controls predominate*, the most likely pupil reactions will be ritualism, retreatism.

(ii) *Utilitarian controls* are unlikely to be predominant by themselves and most likely pupil reactions will be ritualism, retreatism and rebellion.

(iii) *Normative controls* if predominant and positive are most likely to produce reactions of conformity and ritualism, if predominantly negative however, retreatism and rebellion may be prominent.

6 The pupils' adaptation in the class

(i) *Range of adaptation*

	Commitment to subject matter	Responsiveness to presentation	Effort	Disturbance
CONFORMITY	High	High	High	Low-Moderate
RITUALISM	Low	Moderate	Moderate	Low
RETREATISM	Low	Low	Low	High
REBELLION	Low	Low or over-responsive	Low	Low

(ii) *Interrelationship between teachers' control and pupils' response*

CONTROL	RESPONSE
(a) *Coercive controls predominant*:	Ritualism, retreatism
(b) *Utilitarian controls predominant*:	Ritualism, retreatism, rebellion (some conformity)
(c) *Normative controls predominant and positive*:	Conformity, ritualism
(d) *Normative controls predominant and negative*:	Conformity, ritualism but retreatism and rebellion may be present

7 Bibliography

H. O. Dahlke 1958; N. L. Gage 1965; D. E. M. Gardiner 1965; N. Cross 1965; D. Hargreaves 1967; M. E. Highfield 1952; B. Jackson 1964; F. Musgrove 1965; T. Parsons in J. Floud 1961; S. Soles 1964; W. Walker 1932; J. Webb 1962; L. J. Westwood 1966.

XI Relationships between the sociological variables

1 Introduction

So far our analysis of the school society has largely examined each element of the social structure and operation in isolation. In the final chapter of Part Two we combine these analytic variables into a series of propositions which suggest constant and dynamic relationships between them. These propositions are sometimes general, like that which declares that the school's success in attaining goals depends on the relationship between the informal and formal orders, or more specific, like the proposition that the more 'closed' the school society becomes the less normative and coercive kinds of control are distinguishable. These hypotheses originated from a study of the empirical and theoretical literature and have been tested and reshaped in piloting our research and in fieldwork. They refer to residential schools or colleges in particular but most (marked with an asterisk) refer equally well to day schools and all can be profitably considered and reshaped to suit day school conditions.

These propositions are certainly not proven and permanent: they are hypotheses which we are testing and may be validated or otherwise by our research* and then taken up reapplied and retested by others. We publish them here as a focus for thought about the uses of the manual, and as points round which discussion, research or reading can be based to interconnect the previous analytic elements and to render meaningful this study of the school society. The hypotheses are laid out in relation to the main sociological concepts we have introduced. Some are purely theoretical but with profound practical importance to the life and operation of all schools, others are more empirical and a few relate to a part of our own enquiry: the effects of boarding as opposed to day education on similar child populations. In working over these hypotheses and in constructing yet others, both empirical knowledge of schools as

---

*The results of such testing and a discussion of the hypotheses will appear in our main report *Boarding Education: a Sociological Study*.

H*

well as theoretical concepts must be brought together if the resulting statements are to be logically coherent and testable in practice.

With the discussion, research or reading based around and creating further such propositions the sociology of the school comes alive. We have now defined our concepts, laid out the analytic variables of the school's structure and operation, and here we relate them together dynamically, in theoretical propositions which, if validated after thorough testing, explain and predict the resulting empirical situations wherever they may occur. It is these fundamental and general principles governing the operation of societies that sociology is concerned to discover.

2 Some hypotheses for discussion

Goals

1* The society's success in achieving goals depends on the relationship between the formal and informal orders.

2* The greater the emphasis placed on organisational goals, the more difficult is the realisation of the instrumental and expressive goals.

3* The greater the emphasis placed on expressive ends, the less successfully achieved are the instrumental ones, largely because the means for achieving expressive ends are not those most suited to achieving instrumental ones.

4* The greater the stress on organisational goals, the greater is the alienation amongst the pupils from the school's goals as a whole and expressive goals in particular.

5* The greater the emphasis on expressive goals, the greater is the differentiation in role structure. Role conflict in individual role sets (see p. 152) will occur when roles in the expressive and organisational areas are combined, but not necessarily when roles in the expressive and instrumental areas are combined.

Roles

6* When the instrumental and organisational roles in schools are clearly prescribed, the performance of the expressive role is inhibited.

7* Roles performed by adults and pupils in boarding schools will differ greatly from those performed in day schools, family and outside society.

Social Control
8* The more total an institution the wider and deeper are the patterns of adaptation to the structure.
9* In a closed social system normative control is indistinguishable from coercive control.
10* The less pervasive the formal order of social control, the more pervasive the informal order of control and the more difficult becomes deviance from it.
11* To fulfil expressive ends formal control has to be pervasive and normative rather than coercive in nature.
12* Schools which emphasise expressive ends are more total than those which emphasise instrumental or organisational ends.
13* Where the formal social order does not extend the informal social order will exercise its functions.

Authority, Power and Privilege and Sanctions
14* Where the school emphasises expressive ends, there is more congruence between formal authority and informal power.
15* The more differentiated the society is into subsystems the more differentiated are the authority and privilege patterns.
16* Where formal authority and formal privilege are not congruent, alienation will occur amongst the authority holders.
17* Where informal power and formal privileges are not congruent, informal power holders will be alienated from the ends of the institution.
18* The less total the school the less privilege will be used as a reward in the control system.
19* In the instrumental and organisational areas, formal authority alone can be legitimated but in the expressive areas formal authority must coincide with informal power to be legitimated.
20* Where organisational or expressive ends are dominant in a closed institution, staff-type authority and staff-type sanctions will be more widely distributed among the inmates than in a more open institution.

Cultural Expression

21* Real goals and official culture will be less congruent in the expressive and organisational spheres than in the instrumental ones.

22* Where instrumental and expressive ends are dominant in a school, expressive symbols become means of social control, or serve predominantly organisational ends.

Change

23* The more total the school, the greater the pressures for change from outside.

24* Pressures for instrumental change come from without but pressure for expressive and organisational change come from within.

25* Change is most difficult to accomplish in the expressive spheres.

26* The opposition of a role player to a change is proportional to the amount his roles are affected by such a change.

27* The success of a change in the formal order depends on the acceptance of such change by the informal order.

28* When the school is an integral part of a wider social subunit, change is more difficult to accomplish.

Relations with the Outside World

29* The school controls its contact with the outside world to ensure the maintenance of its expressive and organisational systems.

The Informal Social System

30* Where the school places less emphasis on expressive ends the informal order will be more pervasive, homogeneous, total and inescapable.

31* Where the staff are fulfilling organisational roles which are dominant over expressive roles, pupil norms will be hostile to the staff.

32* Where the formal social order is less differentiated, the informal social order will be more total, homogeneous, pervasive and inescapable.

33* The more congruent the formal and informal orders are the more likely are the inmates to identify with staff roles.

34* The more homogeneous the informal social order the more severe its control of deviance from it.

35* The relationship between the formal social order and the informal social order in schools where organisational ends are dominant is suppressive. In schools where expressive ends are dominant it is manipulative and in schools where instrumental ends are dominant it is neutral.

36* Where the formal social order is highly differentiated the informal social order and the formal order will interpenetrate and the more likely is the informal social order to be orientated to the ends of the formal social order.

37* Where the school is an integral part of a subunit of the wider society the reference groups of the pupils are likely to be inside the school and supportive of its ends and organisation. Where the school is not a part of a wider social subunit the reference groups of the pupils are likely to be located outside the school and to be hostile to its ends.

Elites

38* The more custodial the organisation the more informal status is given to alienated groups.

39* Where the norms of the senior pupils conflict with the norms of the school, the norms of the junior pupils will be supportive of the school rather than of the senior pupils.

40* The more custodial the school the more the school attempts to regulate the patterns of association.

41* In the boarding situation patterns of association among pupils are less dependent on the occupation and social class of the parents than in the day school.

42* The more staff roles are distributed amongst the pupils the more fragmented are the patterns of association among the pupils.

Underculture

43 The more total the institution the more diverse is the underculture.

44 The more total the institution the more the underculture compensates for the deprivations imposed by its total nature.

45* Where the school's emphasis on expressive ends and organisation is low the underculture supersedes these functions for the society as a whole.

The Effects of Boarding on Behaviour, Personality, social aspects
46* Where stress is placed on the expressive ends of an institution there will be a greater consensus of attitudes amongst pupils than in schools where the stress is on instrumental or organisational ends.
47* Schools which are part of a wider social system will achieve a wider consensus in attitude among inmates than those not part of a wider subsystem.
48 Schools where authority is widely diffused will produce children who are more authoritarian in behaviour.

Behaviour and Relationships
49 The earlier the age of boarding the more likely the child is to evaluate people in social rather than personal terms.
50* Relationships with people of the same sex in single sex boarding schools will be closer than relationships between the same sexes in coeducational schools.
51 The academic performance of the boarding child of upper and middle intelligence levels will be similar to the performance of day pupils of the same ability. The performance of the less able boarding child will be better, when assessed by external examination, than those of the day child of similar ability.
52* A boarding school with strong expressive goals will be more effective in realising these ends than a comparable day school.

Hypotheses Relating to the Mertonian Paradigm Test
53* In the instrumental areas, there will be no significant difference in response between boarding and day pupils.
54* There will be differences in the expressive sphere between the boarders and day pupils, they will show more ritualism, more conformity and innovation, while the day pupils will show more rebellion and retreatism.
55 In the Public Boarding School the pupils' responses will be more extreme, conformity will be deeper, rebellion greater,

there will be more ritualism, innovation will be more vociferous, retreatism more extreme and eccentric at both staff and pupil levels than in other schools.

The Psychological Adaptations

56 In his relationship with the boarding school the pupil will tend to react to the boarding school environment as a substitute for the family and this may have long-term effects.

57 The age of boarding influences the boarder's affective relationships in depth.

58 Boarders tend to be more gregarious than day pupils.

Sex

59 Boarders from single sex boarding schools find difficulty in responding to the other sex in a natural way on leaving.

Deviance Inside the School

60 The more total the one sex institution the greater is the incidence of deviant sexual adaptations to it.

61* Where the expressive stress and provision of the school is limited deviant sexual adaptations will be more dominant.

62* While there is no evidence that boarding schools produce more homosexuals than day schools it is likely that those that have homosexual and heterosexual tendencies are sensitised more on the homosexual side than in a day school.

63* The informal norms of the society are far more powerful in controlling homosexual relations than the formal norms.

64* In a coeducational situation deviant sexual adaptation is not permitted by either the formal or informal norms.

65 Deviance from the formal norms and values in a total institution may be normal adjustment to norms and values of outside society.

66 In total institutions deviance, which is more common and more extreme than in less total institutions, is counteracted by the formal system with coercive methods.

67* The more total the institution, the more intolerant of deviance is the formal order and the more tolerant the informal order.

68* Wider deviation is tolerated in the expressive sphere than in the instrumental or organisational spheres.

69* The less able child in an academically orientated institution often takes up a deviant adaptation to the society.

The Family

70 Boarding is chosen by some parents because it is a conventional attribute of their pattern of life by others because of abnormalities in their pattern of life and by a middle group who chose if rationally because of upward social mobility.

71 Where boarding has not been part of the parental experience and the child has not experienced primary boarding then parents will claim wider responsibility over the child's life vis à vis the school.

72 The age of first boarding will affect a boy's relationship with parents and siblings. The male boarder will reject mother and boys be closer to father. This is a reversal of day school patterns of family relationships.

73 Severe homesickness in early boarding experience correlates with low academic performance and achievement in the school and cultural fields.

Relations with the Outside World and Home

74 Boarding reduces superficial strains in family relationships but inhibits communications at deeper levels.

75 Boarder's reactions to the home situation and those of parents to the boarder in holiday times are anomic, and the more total the school the more anomic the pattern.

76* Schools with a strong emphasis on expressive ends tend to reject the family as a means of achieving these ends and limit contact with it, whereas schools with low expressive ends admit the primacy of the family in expressive spheres.

77 Where responsibility is assumed by the school over wide areas of the pupils' life contact with the family is severely curtailed.

78 The dispossession of family roles in the boarding situation affects the relationship between siblings both within the boarding school situation and in the family unit.

79 The mode of relationships between parents and child is more affectively neutral amongst the upper classes than amongst the lower income groups.

80 The upper middle class family is less matriarchal than the lower

middle class family and decisions are shared by husband and wife but decisions on boarding may in upper middle class families depend on the mother.

81 In the boarding family the parents are more involved in the wider society.

The Old Boy

82* The more total the institution the more protracted and painful the adjustment to the outside world may be and the less likelihood there is of attaining final adjustment.

83 Boarders will seek to reproduce in outside and later society and in their friendship patterns some features of the norms and values of the schools from which they come.

84* Amongst boarders there is more continuity between the family life when at school and after leaving school than amongst day boys where there is a sharp difference in family life after leaving for a job and achieving economic independence.

Part three
Methodology

1 Methods of investigation

From analysis and hypotheses we turn to the means by which empirical data can be gathered by which to use the analyses and test the hypotheses.

Obviously there are many different methods which might be used, according to the particular focus of the research. The methods of *one* piece of research cannot be automatically applied to another even when the subject matter is germane. Our focus was the contrast between residential and day education and so we are presenting a methodology built around that. Some of it may not apply to other research interests. Much of it however is applicable to day schools, and, for the rest, even if the precise words and construction of tests may need alteration, the principles of the approach will be applicable. It is an essential part of this manual to relate the abstract sociological analysis which we have just completed to a practical methodology, so that the reader has guidelines for gathering data on the sociological issues we have discussed. This is one, though obviously not the only, way of going about it.

Here we give a whole range of methods, interviews, scales, questionnaires and so on. The relevance of most of them to the areas of our analysis will be obvious, but for those questions which are not, we provide cross references back to the sociological sections to which they relate. It must be emphasised that these are the methods which *we* have found useful for studying the school as a society (some of them refer solely to the boarding situation), they are not the *only* methods or necessarily always the best ones for another student's purposes. They are published as guides and suggestions and examples of how .*practically* to collect data for the theoretical analysis we have previously outlined.

To understand this methodology, a word must be said about the nature and design of the research from which it derives. The aim was to make a comparative study of boarding schools as organisations, on the lines we have developed earlier in this book and, also, to attempt to assess the impact of residential or day education on similar populations of children. In all, a sample of seventy boarding schools was chosen and a control group of day schools.* All were studied by observer-participation methods, some, the intensive group of schools, for six weeks or more; the rest for spells of about a week or more. During these stays the following methods' of collecting data were employed.

(i) *Notes of observation.* The researcher kept systematic notes of life in the school and its operation according to the programme provided in this book and methods were standardised among the small research group.

(ii) *Use of documents.* The school usually opened its own files and official and non-official documents, books, records, memoranda, minutes and so on, were used in most schools including much information, whether from Head, staff or pupils, which was confidential and not seen by other groups in the school.

(iii) *Focused interviews in depth.* These interviews, lasting from two to six hours, followed a general plan and were designed to elicit precise information and attitudes but enabled the researcher to explore in detail the operation of the school society. Key members of society were always interviewed in this way: the Head (always at the *end* of a stay), housemasters, some heads of departments, the doctor, matron, bursar, the head boy or girl, heads of houses, selected pupils who were found to be key figures in the formal or informal life: prefects, notable deviants, and so on.

(iv) *Group interviews,* sometimes with staff and with pupils: either written up or tape recorded.

(v) *A systematic three-and-a-half-hour questionnaire* was done only in intensive schools with all senior pupils (about twelve hundred), under examination conditions and in school time. This provides data for most areas of our analysis.

(vi) *Certain standard questionnaires and tests* were completed by the staff interviewed in depth and by others in all schools.

(vii) *Systematic tests and questionnaires* were completed by different groups of pupils in the secondary schools on the extensive sample (by nine thousand pupils); other tests being done in the control day schools and in primary schools.

---

*Methods of choosing and a full account of the procedure are given in *Boarding Education, a Sociological Study* to be published later.

(viii)   *Diaries* recording events and reactions to them were kept by staff and pupils in schools on a voluntary basis.*

(ix)   *Depth interviews* were undertaken with two hundred and seventy parents of a sub-sample of children in the intensive sample. The interview was fairly structured and included tests and questions similar to those applied to the adults and senior children in schools.

The large body of data so collected provides (a) the observer's own data on the day to day working of the school; (b) the evidence of documents not specially prepared for the researcher; (c) the experience attitudes and responses of all sectors of the school society, including parents.

Below we reproduce the notes of guidance which the researchers took to the school. The research group had, of course, previously been instructed in the methodology and difficulties and had worked in partnership in schools to standardise the procedures. The note does not attempt to outline the possibilities and difficulties of observer participation. These will be fully dealt with in our own research report and have been recently discussed, for day schools, by Hargreaves in *Social relations in the Secondary School*.

A checklist of things to do follows—useful to remind the busy researcher of what remains to be done.

2   Procedure in a school (notes of guidance)

(i)   Presumably the headmaster knows what you are doing. As soon as possible after arrival address the staff (if you can) on the research and its purpose. It is absolutely essential to do the same with the senior children (sixth form or top forms)—within a day of arrival. No member of staff should be present at this talk (or talks).

You should tell staff and children that there are no facts about boarding education and this research is trying to gather them, especially to find out (a) the effects of going to boarding schools of different kinds on different children (b) the study of schools as small communities. What are they trying to do, how are they

*For some of this material by pupils see *The Hothouse Society: boarding schools by boarders.*

organised, what do they achieve? What are the differences and similarities between schools?

Stress that this research is based on the boys' and girls' own experience as much as what the headmaster and staff say. Stress this a bit as it gets them interested and undoubtedly encourages co-operation.

Make it clear that you are not a teacher, not an HMI, that though the research is sponsored by the Ministry, the report will be published privately for all to read.

Stress again how their personal experience is important and you have chosen to live in the school rather than whisk in and out with a questionnaire because we believe the boys and girls have much of importance to contribute.

Say that everything will be confidential—no schools will be identified and no individuals. You will not pass any information they give on to the staff or headmaster or vice-versa. You are not a professional sneak. Also you are here to study the school—not to enforce its values. You won't use any of the methods of punishment or enforce the rules.

Outline scope of the research: intensive and extensive surveys of schools. Try and make it clear that this particular school is important for us. Mention that we are also interviewing parents to see what they think the effect of boarding has been on their children and on themselves.

Invite questions.

This talk is often important—to remove misconceptions, get the children's confidence in you, so that they feel you are neither an outside 'official' nor a regular member of staff. Make the whole thing fairly lighthearted with some good jokes (about schools and staff and self-mockery) but very serious when you ask their help. The tone should be that of absolute equality with them: you are inviting them to help you from their unique experience which is important to this study. Make them feel their importance. Give the gist of this to every group you meet in the classroom, even if it means repetition, before doing written work with them.

(ii) Leave interviewing the headmaster until last, by which time you will know a lot about the school. Try not to be seen too much with the headmaster.

(iii) Get round the staff quickly—asking questions of all—so that they feel involved. If you can only interview a few, make the others feel that they are contributing. On no account sit in on their lessons—you are not there reporting on their professional competence—make this clear. Assure staff by word and conduct that you are not spying on them for the headmaster or the governors or the LEA.

(iv) Go through the whole school routine and try and see as much as possible of its life in your stay. Make sure the children see a lot of you—you can do anything to identify yourself with them to do so—join in social activities or have meals with them, etc. It is particularly important to identify with them in ways which the staff do not or cannot—e.g. joining in informal pupil coffee-making at night. It is essential that your conduct should not associate you with the staff or headmaster side of the organisation, or any other role in the school. Keep your independent role as a researcher.

(v) BEWARE of (a) *breaking confidence*—it's so easy and morally difficult if sometimes you find undesirable or downright illegal activity (brutality, etc.). You must not break confidence under any circumstances. (b) *Of being manipulated*. Groups in the school may use you against each other, or children may exploit your immunity to give themselves immunity. Don't allow yourself to be manipulated. (c) *Of making value judgements to others*—you are not here to sport your views, try and be neutral but not inhuman or negative. People respond to warmth and you can wax vehemently on matters not germane to this study (e.g. the merits of Chelsea FC or of Victorian architecture). (d) *Of making value judgements to yourself*: distinguish between your value-laden responses and objective appraisal as laid down in this model. Make sure your modes of observation are objective. If you need an outlet for your value judgements (and remaining neutral and objective is a severe strain), keep a personal diary in which you record your own responses—but this should be distinguished from your objective diary and notes of observation of this research. (e) *Of over-involvement*: a subtle blend of intense interest and complete detachment is required so that, when you leave, you feel able to extricate yourself from those who have so fully helped and opened their lives to you, and they do not feel deceived by the sudden rupture of a confidential relationship. This will present you with severe moral problems. (f) *Of normlessness*. You *must* be normless, to keep your independent role as a researcher, inside but not of this society. But the loss of personal identity is a strain, you are attempting to be an analytic mirror. Your personal diary and trips outside should help you to retain some sense of identity.

Bibliography

The following texts are relevant to the methodology:
P. M. Abell 1969; H. S. Becker 1957, 1958; B. Bernstein 1965; W. A. L. Blyth 1960; A. V. Cicourel 1964; C. Coombs 1953; J. P. Dean 1954; N. Elias 1956; K. M. Evans 1962, 1964; L. Festinger 1953; B. F. Green 1954; P. Hammond 1964; H. Hyman 1954, 1955; P. F. Lazarsfeld 1959; S. M. Lipset 1956; R. K. Merton 1956; J. L. Moreno 1960; C. A. Moser 1958; C. E. Osgood 1957; H. W. Polsky 1962; C. Selltiz 1965; M. Sherif 1964; W. F. Whyte 1955; H. Zetterberg 1954.

3 Methods of obtaining data related to the sociological analysis

These were the guide lines along which the research operated. Next we present for the reader of the manual a tabular analysis which relates the sociological analysis we have previously given to the methodology we are about to give. Thus if the user of this book wishes to see how to go about gathering material on, say, goals or change, the second column will direct him to the relevant questions we asked in the interviews, the third column will give the references to the questions in tests and questionnaires with pupils and the final column suggests other material which we found available in the schools and valuable for the study of the sociological areas in question. The interviews, tests and questionnaires then follow, the purpose and technique of each being explained as it proceeds.

CHAPTER	SECTION	MATERIAL Interviews	Test and Pupil Questionnaire	OTHER
1 GOALS	General	Headmaster q.4, 6, 12, 17, 18 Housemaster q.3, 11, 15, 17 Parents q.24	Questions: 1, 70, 72, 74, 75, 76, 77, 78, 79, 80, 81, 86, 88, 90 Social Adaptation Test	Documents Minutes Speeches Observation Scales of institutional and expressive control
2 SUBUNITS	General	Headmaster q.3, 10, 12 Housemaster q.2, 6, 7, 8,	Questions 6-7, 58, 65-67, 68, 82, 83 Perception of decision-making Staff role sheet Staff-pupil relations sheet	Documents Observations
	Academic	Headmaster q.3, 10, 11, 12, 14 Housemaster q.2	Questions 8-19	Exam results Early leaving
3 CONTROL	Formal	Headmaster q.3, 8, 11, 12, 15, 18, 19 Housemaster q.2, 16, 17 Head of school q.2	Perception of decision-making	Punishment books staff manuals Scale Institutional control Scale Expressive control Observation
	Informal	Parents q.34-41	q.27-30, 72, 74, 75, 77, 89 Informal control	Pupil diaries

CHAPTER	SECTION	MATERIAL		
		Interviews	Test and Pupil Questionnaire	OTHER
4 ADAPTATION AND INFORMAL SOCIAL ORDER	Merton Paradigm	Headmaster q.15, 19 Housemaster q.8, 12, 13	Social Adaptation Test Question 87	Pupil diaries Group discussion
	Informal system	Headmaster q.7, 9, 10, 12, 15, 17, 19 Housemaster q.8, 9, 12, 13, 14, 15, 17 Head of school q.3, 4	Informal control Questions 18, 58, 72, 74, 75, 77, 78, 82, 83, 88, 89, 90	
	Social relations in school	Headmaster Housemaster q.2, 3, 13 Head of school q.3, 4	Staff-Pupil relations q.13, 14, 56, 57, 65-69, 71, 79, 80, 81, 82, 89	
5 ROLES		Headmaster q.2, 3, 4, 5, Housemaster, q.2, 3, 4 Head of school q.2, 3 Parents q.25, 29, 30	Staff Role Sheet Questions 13, 14, 43, 65-69 Staff-pupil relations	Pupil diaries Group discussion
6 CHANGE		Headmaster q.6, 7, 9, 10, 12, 13 Housemaster q.9, 10, 11 Parents q.15	Questions 12, 48, 79, 80, 81, 83 Perception of decision-making	Minute books Documents to parents House record books
7 AUTHORITY, STATUS AND ELITES	Authority	Headmaster q.2, 3, 8, 10, 11 Housemaster q.2, 6, 7 Head of school q.2, 3, 4, 5	Questions 6, 7	School lists duty manuals
	Status Elites		Questions 6, 7, 72, 74-78 Questions 71, 73 Social Adaptation Test	Pupil autobiographies
8 SCHOOL IN THE WIDER SOCIAL SYSTEM		Headmaster q.1, 8, 11, 13, 14 Housemaster q.1, 7 Head of school q.1 Parents q.1-13, 73-87	Questions 20-26, 31-39, 50-52	Scale of institutional control
9 EFFECTIVENESS OF THE ORGANISATION			See relevant chapter for details	

4 Questionnaires and tests

Now we turn to the tests and questions which provided us with part of the information gathered from the pupils. Our sample of schools was divided into two groups, an intensive one and an extensive one.

Six schools were in the intensive group. Here one or more observers lived in the school and for about six weeks. Most members of staff were interviewed and holders of important positions were often questioned on several occasions. Every senior pupil completed a lengthy pupil questionnaire under examination conditions at the end of the observer's stay.

The other schools were visited for a shorter period of about one or two weeks. As many staff as possible were interviewed but special emphasis was given to those positions that the interview schedules outline (headmaster, housemaster, head boy etc.). All pupils of selected ages answered questions in writing during lesson periods given up by staff. Each age group answered a selection of questions from the main questionnaire, especially the goals sheet, q.29, 30, 31, 34, 36, 45, 46, 47, 48, 65, 66, 67, 79, 80, 82, 85, 86, 88, 89.

First we look at the *intensive* study schools where the questionnaire set to senior pupils gives some statistical evidence in testing hypotheses and interrelating sections of the sociological summary. About twelve hundred pupils completed this and from it certain questions were repeated and additional tests made in our *extensive* school sample, these are illustrated after the questionnaire.

(i) Pupil questionnaire This questionnaire was answered by every senior pupil in schools of the intensive sample of schools. It was filled in under examination conditions, to prevent collaboration, at the end of the researcher's stay so that the pupils understood the nature and purpose of the research and in many cases had built up a personal relationship with the researcher.

The questions were similar for all schools, although in some cases, in denominational schools and mixed boarding schools for example, additional questions relevant to the situation were added. The closed questions (e.g. 77, 84, 85, 86) were drawn up from replies to a preliminary pilot questionnaire, while others were designed specifically to test certain hypotheses.

As with the interview schedules those questions relevant to particular areas of the preceding sociological analysis are indicated, although many are self-evident. A short note on coding the questions, that is the system used to count and categorise the answers, concludes this section.

PLEASE READ THIS FIRST

1 This questionnaire is part of the research which I am doing into boarding and day schools and their effects and which has been sponsored by the Ministry of Education since early 1964. A lot has been written on the merits and defects of boarding education but there are still virtually no facts on the matter. Only *you* can provide them for only you are experiencing what it is like to be at a boarding school now. Your help is essential if we are to understand what boarding schools set out to do, how they work and what they achieve. By completing this questionnaire frankly and carefully you will be making a personal contribution to research on a subject of great public interest as well as helping to devise policy in this school and elsewhere.

2 The results will be published in a book. Though the names of schools and individuals will naturally be concealed, every effort will be made to preserve the identities of the people and schools which have contributed to this research. We need general statistics but also individual insights and experience. That is, again, why your help will be so valuable.

3 *The questionnaire is anonymous and strictly confidential. Under no circumstances will anyone in this school—master or boy— be allowed to see your completed answers. Please feel free then to write what you really think.*

4 Please be quite frank but try not to exaggerate. Do not talk or look at your neighbour's answers. Remember, it is *your own* experience and opinions that matter, no one else's.

5 Most questions can be answered quickly by a tick or by adding whatever you think necessary. Some require careful replies in your own words. Please take your time over them. You have 1½ hours for the whole thing. Go through them in order without skipping any.

6 You should find it interesting: after all, it is your chance to say exactly what you think and have experienced on an issue where your experience counts most. I much appreciate your co-operation now and all the other help I have received from so many of you during my stay in this school.

QUESTION 1 :

This test relates to the goals and effectiveness sections of the preceding sociological analysis. After much piloting in schools with heads, staff and pupils, a group of the most frequent goals was constructed, some instrumental, some expressive and some organisational, some mixed. The test attempts to establish the response to these goals: how far they are perceived, or proposed or are felt to be achieved. A simple scoring device is used. The test is used with heads, staff, pupils and parents and proves an effective means of establishing the goal perceptions of different elements of the school community, as well as indicating commitment or alienation and a vital measure of differences between schools. This is particularly the case when responses of different groups or schools are classified according to the instrumental/expressive/organisational categories and then compared. On the test the goals are classified as follows: I = instrumental; I/E = instrumental with expressive connotations; E = expressive; E/I = expressive with instrumental connotations; O = organisational. The test works well with children who like to give the school marks for a change and yet take it seriously. If used with them, it is as well to give an example verbally and score it first.

The test relates to hypotheses 1-5, 11, 12, 13, 17, 20, 21, 22, 29, 30, 35, 45, 46, 52, 67, 76, 89.

Here is a list of some things which this school might be *trying to do* as far as you, the pupils here, are concerned. Go down the list and (1) rank those things which you think it is trying to achieve (2) then rank in the next column those things which you think it *should* try to achieve and (3) in the third column those things which in actual fact it *does* achieve now.

	This school	Does try to	Should try to	Does succeed in doing
cultivate each person's individuality			E	
make life here something like that at home			E	
give everyone the education best suited to his ability			I	

This school	Does try to	Should try to	Does succeed in doing
train leaders for the future		I	
keep the school running efficiently		O	
develop each of us physically		I/E	
put into practice Christian values		E	
prepare us for a democratic society		E/I	
get good O and A level results		I	
maintain firm discipline		O	
develop our critical faculties		I/E	
prepare us for a suitable job or career		I	
teach people to respect each other		E	
keep us occupied most of the time		O	
develop our cultural interests		E/I	
provide experience in managing people		I	
enable us to recognise what is right from what is wrong		E/I	
develop our creative talents		E	
foster a sense of sportsmanship		E	
keep a good reputation outside		O	

Score in this way:

0—5

0 the school doesn't try, shouldn't try, doesn't succeed

1 the school tries to a very small degree, should try to a very small degree, succeeds to a very small degree

2 the school tries to a small degree, should try to a small degree, succeeds to a small degree

3 the school tries to a moderate degree, should try to a moderate degree, succeeds to a moderate degree

4 the school tries to a considerable degree, should try to a considerable degree, succeeds to a considerable degree

5 the school tries to a great degree, should try to a great degree, succeeds to a great degree.

I

QUESTIONS 2, 3, 4, 5:

Provide basic data by which to examine other variables.

2 Your age now: ....years ....months

3 Your age on entry to this school: ....years ....months

4 Present form:

5 House:

QUESTIONS 6, 7:

These questions establish the pupils' participation and status in the system of the school and the subunit of the house. The various offices and positions are given separate scores (e.g. 10 for house captain, 2 for junior soccer team) and the total score for school or house thus expresses the degree and span of involvement of the pupil. This again serves as a useful measure by which to examine other variables, and of comparison between subunits and schools.

The questions relate to the previous sections of the sociological analysis: that on subunits, pupil authority, adaptation and to hypotheses on authority (14, 15, 16, 17, 18, 19, 20, 48).

6 (a) Do you hold any rank in the House now? (e.g. Head of House, Prefect, Sub-Prefect, Special Duties, Squad Leader etc.) (Tick)

> Yes .... Which? ....
> No ....

(b) Have you been captain or in charge of any House game or sport this year? (Tick)

> Yes .... Which? ....
> No ....

(c) Have you been in charge of any other House activity this year? (e.g. music, etc.) (Tick)

> Yes .... Which? ....
> No ....

(d) Have you taken part in any House teams, committees or official activities this year (other than those you were in charge of)? (Tick)
        Yes .... Which? ....
        No ....

7 (a) Are you a School Prefect, School Captain, etc? (Tick)
        Yes .... Specify ....
        No ....

(b) Have you been Captain, Secretary or in charge of any School game this year? (Tick)
        Yes .... Which? ....
        No ....

(c) Have you been in charge or Secretary of any other School activity this year (e.g. a committee, the council, society, group, etc.)? (Tick)
        Yes .... Which? ....
        No ....

(d) Have you taken part in any School teams, the council, committee, choirs or other activities this year (other than those you were in charge of)? (Tick)
        Yes .... Which? ....
        No ....

(e) Have you won any School Colours, Games Colours, prizes or awards this year or signed the Honours Book? (Tick)
        Yes .... Which? ....
        No ....

(f) If you are in the Corps, what rank are you now?
        section: .... rank: ....

If you were in the Corps but have now left, what was your rank on leaving?
        section: .... rank: ....

QUESTIONS 8, 9, 10, 11, 12, 13:

Produce basic data on the academic subunit and on pupil adaptations, as well as comment and criticism of some instrumental goals of schools. They relate to hypotheses 51, 73.

8 Have you taken any 'O' levels yet? (Tick)
        Yes ....   How many?
        No ....   Took.........Passed.........

9 Are you taking any 'O' levels this summer? (Tick)
        Yes .... How many? ....
        No ....

10 What are you main and subsidiary subjects now?
        main: .... subsidiary: ....

11 Which subject (or subjects) do you (a) like best ....
                                     (b) like least.................

12 Do you think that the curriculum (i.e. arrangement and choice of subjects, etc.) needs improvement? (Tick)
        Yes ....
        No .... go on to q.13
If yes:
in what ways?

13 Are you satisfied with the teaching here? (Tick)
        Yes .... go on to q.14
        No ....
If no: Why not?

QUESTION 14:

The first of several carefully scattered questions which examine the pupils' attitudes to teachers: their technical performance, their professional commitment, their interest in their pupils. Answers cross-tabulate significantly with academic performance and social adaptation of pupils. Relevant to the sociological analysis of adaptation, pupil society, staff-pupil relations.

    This one and the questions below refer to hypotheses 51, 53, 69, 73.

14 Which of the following statements fit the staff here? Tick as many as apply.
        Most are good teachers ....
        The majority don't do their job
          properly ....

Most are teachers because they
really believe in the value of
teaching ....

Most are teachers because they
want a good job and salary ....

Most are friendly out of school...........................

Most are not really interested in the
boys ....

Add any comments or qualifications of your own:

QUESTIONS 15, 16, 17, 18, 19:

Provide further basic data on academic aspirations, career expectations and aspirations. They provide data for the goals, academic organisation, adaptations and effectiveness sections of the sociological analysis.

15 Would you like to stay on to the Sixth form here? (Tick)

Yes ....

No ....

16 Would you like to take any 'A' levels?

Here: (Tick)

Yes ....

No ....

Somewhere else: (Tick)

Yes ....

No ....

17 Do you hope to go on to a University or other place for further education or training? (Tick)

Yes ....

No .... go on to q.18 now

If yes:

(a) which four universities (or places of further education) would you most like to go to in order of importance?

1

2

3

4

(b) have you been accepted finally or provisionally by any university or place of further education? (Tick)

Yes .... Which? ....

No ....

18 Which career do you think you will most probably take up?

19 Have you definitely got a job of this kind fixed up yet? (Tick)

Yes..................

No ....

QUESTIONS 20, 21, 22, 23:

Give essential data on the background and assimilation of pupils: the nature of previous education, its congruence with the present school, the degree of assimilation achieved in it (q.22). All this can be compared with the pupils' adaptation in the present school.

They therefore relate to the sociological analysis of the presenting culture, assimilation and status, and to hypotheses 51, 90, 91, 92, 93.

20 How many different schools did you go to from the time you first started going to school until you came here? (Don't include this one)

(a) Age at which first started going to school ....

Number of schools
attended

Primary, Junior (up to 11) ....

Secondary (over 11) ....

Prep or Pre-Prep ....

21 Please give the name, place and type of the school you went to *immediately before coming here*:

(a) Name:

(b) Place:

(c) Type: (Tick which)

Secondary Modern ....

Bilateral/Comprehensive ....

Grammar or Tech. ....

Prep. School ....

Other: ....

22 At your Junior School or Prep School were you (Tick which applies or apply)

     Head of School ....

     Head of House ....

     Prefect (monitor etc.) ....

     Captain of a game ....

Other office:

     Held no office ....

     Can't remember ....

23 Did you pass the 11 + exam? (Tick)

     Yes ....

     No ....

     Don't know ....

     Never took it ....

QUESTION 24:

A crucial question which provides the recollected response to the previous school which can be related to the response to the present one (q.78). The categories can be collapsed for analysis.

    Vital to the study of the presenting culture, adaptation and effectiveness, it also relates to hypotheses 49, 53, 54, 55, 56, 57, 73.

24 Looking back now, how would you say you got on at your Junior/Prep school(s)?

     I thoroughly enjoyed it ....

     I was happy most of the time ....

     I found it tolerable ....

     I enjoyed it at first but not towards

       the end ....

     I was unhappy in the first years but

       happy enough in the last ones ....

     I was unhappy for much of the

       time ....

     I hated it for most of the time..........................

—anything else? ....

              ....

              ....

Please explain *why* you felt this way:

QUESTIONS 25, 26, 27, 28, 29, 30:

All these relate to boarding education only, and examine the age of first boarding, expectations of boarding, homesickness.

25 Were you a boarder or a day-boy in the year immediately before you came to this school? (Tick)

boarder ....

day-boy ....

26 At what age did you first leave home to board in any school?

....

27 Can you describe in your own words how you felt when you first left home to board in any school?

28 In particular, when you left home to board in any school *for the first time* were you (Tick which *one* applies)

homesick for most of the time at
School? ....

homesick a great deal for the first
years? ....

homesick at first but only
occasionally afterwards? ....

homesick only when term started?.......................................

rarely homesick? ....

never homesick? ....

—any additions or comments:

29 What did you expect life at a boarding school such as this to be like before you went to one yourself?

30 Did the life differ in any way from your expectations when you actually started boarding? (Tick)

Yes ....

No ....

If yes: please say how it differed:

QUESTIONS 31, 32, 33, 34, 35, 36, 37:

These give data on the sibling position of the pupil, the marital status of the parents, the educational background of parents and indices of socio-economic class of the parents. Such data is fundamental for most analysis, and most hypotheses (especially 41, 56, 58, 70, 71, 72).

31 Are you: (Tick)
      an only child? .... go on to q.23
      the oldest child of your parents? ....
      the youngest child of your parents? ....
      between youngest and eldest? ....
      a twin? ....

If you have brothers and/or sisters:
Are (or were) they at a boarding school after the age of 11?.........

32 Are your own parents:
              both living now ....
              only mother living ....
              only father living ....
              neither living now ....
              divorced/separated ....
              mother remarried ....
              father remarried ....

33 Have you any relatives who were or are at this school (apart from your brothers)? (Tick)
              Yes ....
              No ....

34 Did your mother go, after the age of 13, to (Tick which)
              a boarding school? ....
              a day school? ....
              don't know? ....

35 Did you father go to (Tick which)
      a state-maintained school as a
      boarder? ....
      a state-maintained school as a
      day-boy? ....
      an independent or private school
      as a boarder? ....
      an independent or private school
      as a day-boy? ....
      don't know ....

36 What is the occupation of your father or your present guardian?
  (a) what sort of work does he (she) do? ....
  (b) in what sort of trade, industry or profession?.................
     r*

37   Whereabouts is your family home now?
     place .... county or country.......................

QUESTIONS 38, 39, 40:

Explore the pupils' pattern of holiday living, his mobility, and the degree of identification with the neighbourhood. The latter question (40) compares with later ones on friendships, and the home.
     Relevant to the presenting culture, school and society, and hypotheses 70, 71, 75, 82.

38   Is this where you spend most of your holidays? (Tick)
              Yes .... go on to q.39
              No ....
if no:
with whom do you normally spend your holidays? (Tick which applies)
              parent(s)? ....
              guardians? ....
              other relatives? ....
              friends? ....
              others? ....

39   Have you moved home since you first came here? (Tick)
              Yes .... how many times?
              No ....

40   How do you get on with the neighbourhood at home (or in the place where you usually spend most of your holidays)? (Tick)
              I feel very much a part of it..............................
              I feel that I belong there ....
              I sometimes feel a bit out of things.......................
              I feel a bit of a stranger ....
              I have very little to do with it ....

Anything else:

QUESTIONS 41, 42, 43:

Explore further the pupils' involvement in the outside peer culture, and the pattern of life at home. From these facts useful checks emerge on later attitudes (e.g. religion), internal deviance inside the school, patterns of association and roles outside the school (to compare with those inside).

The questions provide valuable data for the sections on goals, roles, adaptation and culture, the school and socicty, as well as the effectiveness of schools. Relevant hypotheses are 7, 75.

41 Have you any really close friends (i.e. someone you could discuss personal problems with) of your own age at home? Tick whichever applies (apply).

> Yes, from this school ....
> Yes, not from this school ....
> No ....

42 Have you a girl-friend there now? (Tick)
> Yes ....
> No ....

43 During the last holiday did you—(tick only those that apply)

Yes

> go to church once or twice
> or occasionally ....
> go to church regularly once a
> week or more ....
> smoke at all ....
> drink any intoxicants ....
> go out with a girl-friend ....
> spend an afternoon or more with
> someone who was at this school
> last term ....
> go to a club or society near home ....
> go to or give a teenage party near
> home ....
> see quite a lot of some friends near
> home ....
> do a paid job ....

QUESTION 44:

Provides a factual check on the control and values exercised by the home, to be compared with that exercised by the official system of the school. (Relevant to school and society.)

44 Some parents (or guardians) have 'rules' for their children and others do not. Tick any items below about which your parents (or guardians) have 'rules' or an understanding with you during the holidays. (Tick only those that apply)

a time for being in at night ....

against smoking ....

against drinking intoxicants ....

against seeing too much of the

other sex ....

about going to church regularly ....

about doing a certain amount of

school work ....

Any others:

QUESTIONS 45, 46, 47:

Provide material on relationships within the family unit and reaction to living at home. When collapsed the reactions can be cross-tabulated with other important variables.

They relate therefore to the sections on adaptation, school and society and the presenting culture and to hypotheses 29, 56, 57, 70, 72, 74, 75, 78, 79, 80, 84, 86.

45 How do you find you get on when at home with

your mother your father your brothers

(or guardian)   and/or

sisters

we get on very well

we get on fairly well

things are tolerable

relations are sometimes

strained

relations are often diffi-

cult

we don't get on at all well

additions:

(Put a tick in each section that applies to you)

46 Has going to a boarding school affected your relationship with your family in any way? Please answer fully in your own words:

47 How do you find living at home during the holidays? (Tick)
    I enjoy it very much and wish I
    could be there far more ....
    I like being there throughout the
    holidays ....
    It's all right but I'm glad to get
    back to school when term starts......................
    I like being there for some of the
    holidays but not all ....
    I find it a bit of a strain for much
    of the time ....
    I don't like being there much ....
    I'd honestly rather be there as
    little as possible ....
Anything else?
Please give the reasons for your answer:

QUESTIONS 48, 49, 50:

These concern boarders and their relations with response to the home and their parents' wishes in sending them away to school.

48 Could you sum up here the advantages and disadvantages of living away from home during term?
    (a) list the *advantages for you* in living away from home:

    (b) list the *disadvantages for you* in living away from home:

49 For what reasons do you think your parents (or guardians) sent you to school here?
    1
    2
    3
    4

50   Have you seen or do you expect to see any relatives here this
term (apart from any who are pupils)? (Tick)
        Yes   ....
        No ....
        Don't know ....

QUESTIONS 51, 52, 53, 54, 55, 56, 57:

Besides giving yet further data on peer associations both within
and outside or based on the school, these questions are some
of several which explore reactions to the opposite sex.

They relate thus to the sections on adaptation, patterns of
association, sexual adaptations and school and society. The
data on the opposite sex correlates with that gained from the
Thematic Apperceptions test which we used and that based
on Merton's paradigm, page 295. It also refers to hypotheses
57, 59, 60, 61, 62, 74.

51   Have you any close friends of your own age and sex near here
(apart from boys actually at this school now)? (Tick)
        Yes, connected with the school ....
        Yes, not connected with the school ....
        No ....

52   Have you a girl-friend near here at present (apart from one
you may have at home)? (Tick)
        Yes   ....
        No ....
If yes:
Roughly how often do you see her? .... per ....

53   Do you think that the senior boys at this school (Tick *which*
one)
        see too much of the other sex ....
        see about enough of them ....
        see too little of them? ....
Anything else:

54 What about *you* personally:
Would you like to have more to do with girls here if it were possible? (Tick)

Yes ....

No ....

Don't know ....

55 Which of the following most nearly describes your own reaction when in the company of a girl? (Tick)

I'm usually quite at ease ....

I look self-confident but don't feel
it ....

I tend to put on a bit of a show ....

I feel a bit embarrassed ....

I feel uneasy ....

Any alternatives or additions:

56 Has being away from girls and women had any effect on your attitudes or reaction to them?

57 In your experience are there any good or bad effects produced by living in a community all of your own sex?

(a) the good effects:

(b) the bad effects:

QUESTIONS 58, 59, 60, 61, 62:

Question 58 provides data on activities which can be used to contrast with perceived goals, the official culture and to build up a picture of adaptations and the culture of the pupil society.

The questions 59-62 are concerned to establish facts and responses to privacy or lack of it in boarding schools only. The relevant hypothesis is 58.

58 What is your favourite way of spending your time

(a)   in out-of-class activities in school:

(b)   when your time is completely your own:

59 Is there anywhere you sometimes go to get away from school for a bit? (Tick)

Yes   ....

No   ....

If yes:
where?
why?

60 How long are you alone on an average weekday—(except for when you are asleep)? (Tick)

five minutes or less ....

more than 5 minutes but less than
15 minutes ....

more than 15 minutes but less than
half an hour ....

more than half an hour but less
one hour ....

more than one hour but less than
two hours ....

more than two hours alone ....

61 Would you like more time alone? (Tick)

Yes   ....

No   ....

If yes:
Why?

62 If you really wanted to be absolutely alone, sometime, where abouts would you go

(a)   inside the school:

(b)   outside the school?

QUESTIONS 63, 64:

Important questions. It is useful to distinguish the general from
the specific problems, as one question tends to produce only
the general one.

The rich data these questions provide relate to the whole
of the sociological analysis, and, especially to pupils' adaptations and the effectiveness of the school. They, and the questions down to 69, test hypotheses 30, 31, 33, 36, 42, 44, 45, 95.

63   What things in general do you worry about most?

64   Life anywhere gives us all problems. What are the most important personal problems *for you* which are caused mainly by life
here?

QUESTIONS 65, 66, 67, 68, 69:

These examine with whom personal problems of increasing
intimacy are discussed within the school society. Similar questions can be asked for the society outside. The answers relate
to expressive goals, the role patterns and the effectiveness of
the schools' staff-pupil relations, pastoral care, patterns of
association and the relationship between formal and informal
orders. Q. 68-69 take this further with the holder of the cardinal
pastoral role in the official system, and those who may develop
similar roles unofficially.

65   If you were seriously disturbed about your work, with whom
(if anyone) in the school would you talk it over?
    with   ....
    with no one............(tick)

66   Supposing grave domestic difficulties developed at home which
troubled you (e.g. your parents were separating), with whom (if
anyone) in the school would you talk it over?
    with   ....
    with no one............(tick)

67 If you were really worried about an intimate personal problem (e.g. of an emotional or moral kind), with whom (if anyone) in the school would you talk it over?

with ....

with no one .... (tick)

68 How close has been your personal contact with your House-master and your Tutor? (Tick which applies)

	H.M.	Tutor
I have got to know him really well as a person	....
I have got to know him fairly well as a person	....
Our contact has been chiefly confined to discipline or formal meetings	....
I scarcely know him as a person	....
We have virtually nothing to do with each other	....

Anything else?

69 Are there any other adults here whom you have got to know well as people? (Tick)

Yes .... Specify ....

No ....

QUESTION 70:

The question assembles characteristics of pupils related to goals. The characteristics are mainly paired opposites but are scattered (e.g. hard working, do a bare minimum of work). It gives an individual pupil's profile of the rest of the pupil society. When aggregated we gather the pupil society's profile of itself: valuable comparisons between school subunits can be made from this. According to the pupil's predominating positive or hostile evaluation of his contemporaries, we also establish data on his relationship with the peer culture and when all the pupils' responses are considered, on associations within the pupil society and patterns of adaptation to it. Individual items (religion, work, games, culture) give material on goals and their realisation. The question, along with others, gives data on goals, official structure, subsystems, pupil society, patterns of association and effectiveness. The answer should be related to that of questions 15 and 19 in the staff questionnaire, and questions 12, 13, 17 in those of head and housemaster. It refers to hypotheses 30, 43, 67, 69, 86.

70 Which of the following statements would fit the majority of boys here? Tick as many as apply.

      reasonably hard working ....

      mainly interested in themselves..........................

      keen on games ....

      friendly   ....

      do a bare minimum of work ....,..................

      hard to get to know ....

      generally active in out-of-class
         affairs   ....

      not interested in cultural things..........................

      keep to the rules...

      preoccupied with girls ....

      cliquey   ....

      cultured   ....

      insensitive   ....

      anxious to get round the rules............................

      fairly good Christians ....

      out for a good time ....

Anything else?

QUESTIONS 71, 72:

One of several questions of a sociometric nature. From it basic clusters can be established.

    Along with the following question, it is relevant to the pupil society, patterns of association and hypotheses 38, 40, 41, 42, 50.

71 Are there any particular boys you go around with most? (Tick)

Yes ....

None in particular ....

If yes:

(a) specify which House(s) they belong to:

(b) what have you got in common (e.g. what sort of things do you like doing together)?

72 Is there any type of boy or group of boys here which you dislike?

(a) none in particular .... (tick) go on to q.73

(b) describe the type of group and give the reasons for your dislike:

QUESTION 73:

Along with interview questions, this helps to identify elites, and the components of status in the pupil world. It is relevant therefore to pupil association and effectiveness in achieving goals.

73 If a new boy arrived here and asked you which group of boys were most prominent *in your age group* in the school (i.e. those who really set the tone or trends or are looked up to), which group (if any) would you mention to him?

(a) none in particular .... (tick)

(b) which group and what makes them prominent?

QUESTIONS 74, 75:

These explore further the constituents of informal status or lack of it, as well as norms of the pupil world. By comparing the results of these (and later questions) with interview and other material from the staff, it is possible to see how the values and status system of the pupil world correspond with those of the staff and official order.

The data is relevant therefore to goals, effectiveness, assimilation, and informal order and to the hypotheses numbered 10, 30, 32, 33, 34.

74 What things about a boy make him *popular* with the other boys here? Tick off the most important things on the list below or add your own.
A popular boy will be:

easy to get on with ....
good at games ....
with a sense of humour ....
reasonably good-looking ....
not *too* good at any one thing ....
generous ....
clever but not hard-working ....
genuine ....
unconcerned about breaking rules ....
one for the girls ....
no respecter of authority ....
well-dressed ....
full of House spirit ....
Anything else?

75 What things about a boy make him *unpopular* with the other boys here? Tick off the most important things on the list below or add your own.
An unpopular boy will be:

officious ....
unwilling to join in things.................................
a hypocrite ....

weak physically ....
a bolsh (or rebel) ....
interested mainly in himself ....
no respecter of authority ....
one who greases up to masters ....
unattractive physically ....
a culture vulture ....
too keen on his own sex ....
one who works too hard ....
poor at sport ....
conceited ....
Anything else?

QUESTION 76:

Relates to hypotheses concerning boarding and its impact: impact in sensitising pupils collectively or individually, compared with similar pupils in day schools. Qualities 1, 4, 6, 8 are collectively-oriented qualities, but 2, 3, 5, 7 are individually-oriented ones. A plus-minus scoring scale allows the result to be expressed as a score. The goals listed in question 1 also can be grouped along this dimension.
Relates to goals, effectiveness, adaptation and hypothesis 49.

76 Which *four* of the following qualities do you personally like to see in a person? (Tick only four)
ability to mix easily ....
imagination ....
sensitivity ....
ability to give a lead ....
independence of mind ....
willingness to co-operate ....
originality ....
tolerance ....

QUESTION 77:

Provides data on informal order, particularly informal norms, deviance from them, controls and outcasts. The terms are derived from piloting in boarding schools. Hypotheses relevant are 10, 30, 68.

77 What are the three worst things that can be said of a boy here by the others? Tick *three* of the following items or add your own.

a boor ....

a snob ....

a weed ....

a yob ....

a sneak ....

a queer ....

a bolsh (or rebel) ....

a slacker ....

a traitor ....

a big-head ....

Additions:

QUESTION 78:

Corresponds with question 24, and is basic to adaptation and for cross-tabulating data on the effectiveness of the school. Relevant to goals, adaptation, effectiveness and hypotheses 1, 54, 55.

78 How have you enjoyed your years at this school? On the whole have you (Tick *one* or add your own)

thoroughly enjoyed being here? ....

had a reasonably pleasant time here? ....

enjoyed it at first but not recently? ....

been happy in the last years but not so in the earlier ones? ....

had a tolerable time? ....

been unhappy much of the time? ....

disliked being here most of the time? ....

really hated it here most of the time? ....

Any alternatives or comments:

Questions 79, 80, 81:

Provide data on adaptations, pressures and change.
Relevant to goals, change, adaptation and effectiveness and hypotheses 1-5, 23-25, 53-55.

79 What are the things you most like about being at this school? *Say why.*

80 What are the things you most dislike about being here? *Say why.*

81 Would you like to see any changes made here? (Tick)
       Yes ....
       None in particular ...... go on to q.82
If yes:
List the most important changes you would like to see:

Question 82:

A ranking question which establishes the pupils' own priorities of satisfaction compared with the official goals, structures, and values, It provides important data on goals, the subsystems, staff-pupil relations, control and effectiveness of schools in general, and is a useful tool for comparisons between schools. Relevant to hypotheses 1-5, 53-55.

82 Which of the following aspects of life here have you personally found most rewarding? Select *three* and put 1, 2 and 3 beside them in order of importance.
    the teaching ....
    opportunities for sport and games ....
    organising and running things ....
    living all the time with other boys ....

contact with some individual
    masters ....
opportunities for drama, music, the
    arts ....
living to a regular pattern ....
relationships with a few boys ....
being able to get round the rules........................

QUESTION 83:

Basic aspects of the school (boarding ones) are isolated and
the pupils indicate their degree of satisfaction with them. The
results give an index of the areas and direction of change required by the pupil society with which to compare that indicated
by staff and others. By adding the ticks in the column 'about
enough now?' one achieves a useful score of satisfaction. This
is useful for cross-tabulation and for comparisons with schools
possessing similar features.

Relevant to goals, subunits, control, authority, the school and
society, adaptation and effectiveness and hypotheses 1-5, 23-25,
53-55.

83 What is your attitude towards the following aspects of school
life? Put a tick in the appropriate section.

Is there	About enough now?	too little (too few)?	too much (too many)?
1 Unbroken time for work			
2 Private study periods			
3 Free time in the school			
4 Freedom outside the school			
5 Team games			
6 Individual games			
7 Privacy			
8 Privileges			
9 Rules			
10 Uniform dress			
11 Compulsory religion			
12 House centredness			

84. Would you like to see any alterations in the religious provision in this school? (Tick)

   Yes ....

   No ....

If yes: what?

QUESTION 85:

Enables aspirations of pupils to be compared with official goals and values, provides data on the value system of the informal order and is a tool for establishing differences between schools or subunits or age groupings.

 Relevant to goals, relations of formal to informal order, adaptations, effectiveness, hypotheses 1-5, 21-22, 36, 43.

85 If you could be *one* of the following here, which would it be?

(Tick only *one*)

   an outstanding sportsman ....

   a leading school prefect or officer ....

   an outstanding scholar ....

   an outstanding actor, musician,

    writer or painter ....

QUESTION 86:

This has multiple purposes. Some items cross-check with some of the goals said to be achieved in question one. Others cross-check and elaborate on the profile of other pupils provided in question 70 and other questions. The whole is composed of pairs of opposed qualities (e.g. leadership, the herd instinct) alleged in our pilot work to be fostered by schools and boarding experience. The pairs are scattered with some single items added. The results provide thus one more indication of the pupils' assessment of the effectiveness of their schools in achieving ends, and of aspects of their society. It provides valuable data for comparisons between schools.

 Relevant to goals, subsystems, control, pupil society, adaptation and effectiveness, and hypotheses 1-5, 43, 60-62.

86 Which of the following do you honestly think being here promotes?
    1 self-reliance and independence ....
    2 the herd instinct ....
    3 the habit of working thoroughly.......................
    4 snobbery ....
    5 Christian life and values ....
    6 service to the community ....
    7 concern for other people ....
    8 frustration ....
    9 interest in cultural things ....
    10 homosexuality ....
    11 respect for truth ....
    12 too much worry about power ....
    13 breadth of mind ....
    14 lack of knowledge of the outside
       world ....
    15 *excessive* concern with girls ....
    16 qualities of leadership ....
    17 too much concern with getting
       qualifications ....
    18 individuality ....
If you wish to expand on any of the above please do so on the
following page in the space provided.

QUESTION 87:

Along with other more elaborate tests (the Thematic Apperception ones, the Merton paradigm ones, etc.) this question pro-
duces data on the collective and individual orientation of the
pupils. Qualities 1, 3, 4, 7 have a collective stress, but 2, 5, 6, 8
are more individually oriented. The question again helps test
the hypotheses on the effects of different styles of boarding (see
Q.76). A plus-minus scale enables the result to be expressed in
a score.
    Relevant to goals, adaptation and effectiveness, it tests hypo-
thesis 48.

87   We all respond to situations in our own way. Which *four* of the following guides to action would *you* follow as a general rule (admitting that there will be exceptions).

As a general rule I would—

put up with things and not grouse
too much   ....

not worry too much about offend-
ing other people's views ....

respect traditional moral standards......................

follow orders without asking the
whys and wherefores ....

question those in authority over
me ....

alter things and not worry about
precedents ....

put the interests of the group before
myself ....

never accept anything as true with-
out thoroughly criticising it first ....

QUESTION 88:

This is an adaptation of standard attitude tests (the Californian F scale etc.). It has multiple purposes. In detail the items (e.g. religion, culture, staff-pupil relations) can be compared with goals and give another measure of goal-effectiveness. Clusters of attitudes provide data on the pupil society and its norms. The span of response (strongly agree—strongly disagree) gives a measure of commitment and degree of reaction as between different communities (relevant to hypotheses on feeling and self-assertion in communities).

The scale provides data on the values of the pupil society, the degree of consensus existing among it, and indications of adaptations to expressive control and real goals. The whole also establishes differences between groups or schools with different expressive aims and class composition etc.

The results can be reduced to a score by counting all the ticks in the 'strongly agree' columns, except those numbered 6, 7, 19, 20. These are 'unorthodox' statements, while the others are more 'orthodox'. Nos. 6, 7, 19, 20 are added to the score if they are ticked under 'strongly disagree' or 'disagree'. The resulting score is a measure of the acceptance of traditional or 'orthodox' attitudes. The summary score is useful for cross-tabulations. It tests hypotheses 1-5, 46-48.

88 Here is a selection of controversial statements on several subjects. Do you agree or disagree with each of them? Put a tick in the appropriate section.

	Strongly agree	Agree	Disagree	Strongly disagree	Don't know
There is a life after death	1.				
Religion is the basis of all true morality	2.				
Christianity is the highest form of religion	3.				
Coloured people are inferior to others	4.				
It is wrong to have sexual relations before marriage	5.				
There's nothing wrong with family life in this country	6.				
Capital punishment should be abolished	7.				
Teenagers in general have too much money	8.				
Women are best kept in the home	9.				
Intellectuals can't be trusted	10.				
Most modern art is unintelligible	11.				

Most pop music is worthless	12..
Television is a menace	13..
Most modern drama is sordid	14..
The best relaxation is still a good book	15..
You can't really read poetry for pleasure	16..
The welfare state is making people soft	17..
We should keep the independent nuclear deterrent	18..
There's not much wrong with this country	19..
Nationalisation is better than free enterprise	20..
There's not much wrong with the Public School system	21..
Schools should be run democratically	22..
Games do mould character	23..
You shouldn't be too friendly with the staff	24..
Beating should be abolished	25..
School uniform should be abolished altogether	26..

QUESTION 89:

A valuable question for establishing the norms which govern the informal order. It can be modified to suit different age groups or structures to elicit precise kinds of norms—e.g.

'what a person should/shouldn't do about' dress, the staff, sex, work, etc. The relevant hypotheses are 30-37, 39, 65.

89 Suppose you have a younger brother aged 13 and he is entering this school next term. He already knows the school and house rules. But what else should he know? Tell him frankly what he *should do* and what he *shouldn't do* if he is to have a tolerable time here. List at least *four* of the most important things under each heading.
To have a tolerable time here he should:
1
2
3
4
5
To have a tolerable time here he should *not*:
1
2
3
4
5
6

90 What would be the best thing that could happen to you at this school this year?
If there is anything not covered in this questionnaire that you would like to add, please do so here:

(ii) Coding the questionnaire The completed questionnaires have now to be coded, that is the replies must be classified and counted. For a full study of coding methods and other analytical techniques reference should be made to C. Moser's *Survey Methods in Social Investigation*, but the uninitiated student might benefit from the following simple illustrations of coding processes.

Closed questions, that is where answers are provided and the respondent ticks those which apply, can be easily counted, but for open questions, that is where the respondents' own answers are written in, a list of coding categories must be drawn up. These coding categories should be based on the theoretical framework outlined in Part Two of this manual, be related to the hypotheses and should be comprehensive enough to admit the differing emphases in the answers of all schools.

Let us suppose for example, that the aim of question 49 is to examine whether the parental reasons for sending their children to particular types of school are related to the goals those schools pursue. The replies to the question 'For what reason do you think your parents sent you to this school' can be broadly classified into Instrumental and Expressive reasons, following our theoretical typology of goals. Attitudes to specific goals or groups of goals may provide additional support for our hypotheses on the family, particularly hypotheses 70, 80 and 81, which are more fully explored in parent interviews.

A coding frame is drawn up which classifies the replies and translates these categories into figures for rapid counting. The numbers are punched on to cards which may then be fed into a computer or counter sorter.

Note	*Instrumental Reasons*		*Code*
	No other good schools/too far away	0	Column 1
Hyp. 70	Better or good education/ 'O' 'A' levels	1	
	Better working conditions/facilities	2	
Hyp. 70	Help one get on in the world/schools reputation	3	
Hyp. 70	Status reasons/the done thing	4	
Hyp. 70	Easier at home if absent/illness, orphan, divorce	5	
Hyp. 70	Parents mobile/abroad/professional	6	
Hyp. 81	Develops special talent or vocation/meets a specialised need/deaf etc.	7	

Expressive Reasons

	Promotes independence/self reliance	8	
	Learning to be with others/social reasons	9	
	It is a free/happy school	0	Column 2
	Religious/moral reasons	1	

Other Reasons Stated

Hyp. 70	Family connections with the school	2	

Other Reasons Stated

Hyp. 70 Parents went to a similar school   3
        I chose to go to this school   4
        Recommended by previous school   5
        Parents wanted to get rid of me   6
Hyp. 80 My mother/father thought it would be good
        for me   7
        They wanted to get rid of me   8
        Don't know   9

The hypotheses which individual sets of replies might illustrate are noted above on the left hand side but obviously are not part of the coding frame.

Hypothesis 70. A boarding school is chosen by some parents because it is a conventional attribute of their patterns of life, by others because of abnormalities in their pattern of life and by a middle group who choose it rationally because of upward social mobility.

Hypothesis 80. The upper middle class family is less matriarchal than the lower middle class family and decisions are shared by the husband and wife but decisions on boarding in upper middle class families depend on the mother.

Hypothesis 81. In the boarding family the parents are more involved in the outside society.

The example given above is a *multi-code,* that is, several replies from each individual are counted, but *summary-codes,* which as their name implies summarise the more detailed categories, can be drawn up. One item is coded, in the case of Question 49 what the respondent sees as the predominant reason for his parents' choice of school. Such codes can be used in *cross-tabulation,* where replies to different questions can be precisely compared. It may be significant, for example, to see whether the parental reasons for choosing particular schools relate in any way to the goals those schools actually pursue, or can the social class of parents be related to particular goal expectations or attitudes to the school. Cross-tabulation allows the testing of many hypotheses.

Bibliography

The following texts are relevant to questionnaire construction, coding and analysis:

L. Festinger 1954; G. Lindsey 1954; H. H. Hyman 1955; C. A. Moser 1958; A. N. Oppenheim 1966; S. L. Payne 1951.

(iii) The extensive sample of schools The previous questionnaire could only be attempted in those schools where observer participation had built up trust in all members of the organisation. This was a job of many weeks and in the schools which made up the extensive sample the stay of the observer was much shorter, varying from a week to three weeks, although in many cases two or more observers were together in the school during the chosen period. Our aim in the schools was to repeat those questions which we felt to be crucial to the understanding of the effects of different organisational structures, to complete as many interviews and penetrate as deeply as possible the informal society in the shorter time allowed. The following notes guided the observers:

Establish a role profile of:
(a) the headmaster
(b) the housemaster (or boarding staff)
(c) Heads of Departments
(d) Assistant master
(e) School Prefects
(f) Professional staff—Chaplain
                              Doctor
                              Bursar
(g) Domestic staff—clerical
                        organisational
(h) Other pupils of different ages

Establish
(1) The objectives of the boarding school as seen by different groups
(2) The official status and culture, the informal value system—underculture, aspirations and adjustment of children

(3) Formal structure as a boarding community and its mode of operation (look especially at distribution of power and sanctions, the status system and the mode of communication—refer to printed sheet).

Methods:

(1) Observe as much as you can—sit in on meetings, examine notice boards, etc.; write up description of the place

(2) Interview key figures: headmaster, some housemasters, some staff, a matron, the head boy, the doctor

(3) Get children in class to write you things:
   (i) Diaries, reports
   (ii) Questions from questionnaires

(4) Collect and examine documents: Prospectus
   Notes for new masters
   Rules
   Timetable
   Magazines
   Lists and notices from boards
   Unofficial documents

(5) Talk to children singly or in groups

(6) Apply scale of institutional control

(7) Summarise school on analytic framework

(iv) Written work from children in extensively studied schools
One part of the methodology was the answering of questions and tests by children in the extensive sample of schools. Each age/intelligence group was asked identical questions in different schools, the questions being taken from the questionnaire applied in the intensive sample of schools, or specially designed. References to questions are to those in the intensive questionnaire given previously.
All pupils to write: (i) Diaries

   (ii) Basic data: Age, sex, number of brothers and sisters, father's and mother's education (boarding/day), name of home town or village, day pupil/boarder.

First form: How school differed from what expected
               Pastoral care questions qq.65, 66, 67
Fourth form: Aspirations q.85
               Norms q.89
               Advantages and disadvantages of living away from
                  home q.48
               Staff-Pupil relations
               Reference group, friends at home
Fifth form: Aspirations q.85
               Norms q.89
               Social adaptation test (Merton test)
               Staff-pupil relations
               Goal sheet q.1
               What school promotes q.80
               What found rewarding q.82
               Family relations qq.45, 46
               Neighbourhood relations q.47
Lower Sixth: Psychological apperception tests
               Staff-pupil relations
               Norms q.89
               Merton adaptation test
               Advantages and disadvantages of living away from
                  home q.48
               Reference group, friends at home
               Goal sheet q.1
               Family relations qq.45, 46
               Neighbourhood relations q.47
Upper Sixth: Goal sheet q.1
               Merton adaptation sheet
               Pastoral care qq.65, 66, 67
               Staff-pupil relations
               Advantages and disadvantages of boarding q.48
               Attitudes q.88
               School promotes q.86
               What found rewarding q.82

Besides repeating the questions given in intensive schools, some
specially devised ones were set.

First, in order to gather quantitative material, about communication and change and especially the perception of decision making

and therefore of the power structure of the school, the following test was applied.

(*a*) *Perception of decision-making.* In any school there are certain decisions which must be made if things are to run smoothly.

Here is a list of decisions of different types. Who would you say was responsible in this school for making each of these sorts of decisions?

Then at the end give a score for the amount of influence you think senior pupils have on the decision when it is made:

1 No influence at all
2 Very slight influence
3 Moderate influence
4 Large amount of influence
5 Completely their decision
x Don't know

	Who makes decisions	Score for influence of senior pupils
School rules (going out, uniform etc.)	....	....
Organisation (daily routine etc.)	....	....
Academic (subjects, timetable)	....	....
Social life (societies, outings)	....	....
Games (fixtures, admin.)	....	....
Teams (picking sides)	....	....
Catering (menu, tuck shop)	....	....

Secondly, to establish the nature and strength of controls used by the pupil society, we used the following questions to compare with interview and observational material.

(*b*) *Informal control.* If a boy in your age group told a member of staff that certain boys had been breaking school rules, with the result that your whole form was punished (e.g. gated or sent to bed early, etc. or privileges withdrawn):

(1) What action if any would *you* yourself be likely to take with the boy regarding his behaviour in telling the staff?

(2)   What action, if any, is it likely the other boys *as a group* would take with the boy regarding his behaviour in telling the staff?

The third question attempts to quantify the degree of contact by the pupil with different members of staff and in different areas of school life.

(*c*)   *Staff-pupil relations.* How close is your contact with the staff? Below are several aspects of your life here and the positions of several people whom you come into contact with regularly. Go through the list and score for the closeness of the relationship you have had with each of the people in your time here.

(1)   Hostile relations, very distant contact
(2)   Distant, formal routine relations
(3)   A bit more informal than with most other staff here
(4)   Very informal relations
(5)   Very informal and friendly
(x)   Have had no relationship at all in this area

With	Housemaster	Assistant housemaster	Chaplain	Matron	Subject master	Games staff
In your work						
In games and sport generally						
In the school's religious life						
In cultural life						
In the way you are looked after materially						
In your personal welfare and problems						

Next we devised, after much testing, a measure of the pupils' adaptations to various parts of the school's structure or values: authority, religion, academic work, games, culture, reputation. These can be clustered into groups according to their instrumental, expressive and organisational nature. The adaptations examined are those suggested in the paradigm of R. K. Merton: conformity, ritualism, innovation, retreatism and rebellion. The responses A—E reflect these adaptations but are randomly distributed thus:

Question	1	2	3	4	5	6
Conformity	A	C	B	A	A	A
Ritualism	C	D	A	D	E	E
Innovation	D	E	E	E	B	D
Retreatism	B	B	C	B	D	B
Rebellion	E	A	D	C	C	C

Besides testing adaptations, the question supplements and cross-checks other data gained: e.g. on loyalty (see no. 6) on religion and so on. The relevant hypotheses are 53-55.

This questionnaire is very popular with pupils and is useful as a start to a session with them. They think seriously about it and take considerable time completing it.

(*d*) *Social adaptation test.* Below you will find a number of situations described—and after each situation five possible reactions. Decide which one of these reactions is most typical of you and write the appropriate letter in the square provided. Obviously there are no right answers. Work quickly, and try to be completely honest about yourself. *Choose one reaction only*, the one you would actually have, and not the ones you would like to have.

1 You have been made a prefect. Would you:
  (a) Do your best
  (b) Do as little as possible
  (c) Even if you don't like the school's policy, make sure that everyone keeps the rules
  (d) Enforce only the rules you believe are valuable
  (e) Don't worry about the rules, exploit the position for what it is worth

2 You are working for an exam. The master tells the form to work much harder, would you:
  (a) Don't give a damn either for the exam or for the master
  (b) Just continue to do a sufficient amount to keep out of trouble
  (c) Realise that this is important and work harder
  (d) Carry on as before and hope you will be lucky in the exams
  (e) Make sure you will pass the exam but don't worry about working harder in his class

3   There is a voluntary chapel service. The headmaster on this
    occasion urges all to attend. Would you:
    (a) Go, and take a book to read
    (b) Go, because it might be rewarding
    (c) Have a headache and don't go
    (d) Refuse to go, you don't believe in it anyway
    (e) Don't go to this service but continue to think over religious
         issues

4   You are selected for a school first team for an important match.
    Would you:
    (a) Play well and try to win
    (b) Say you don't want to play
    (c) Don't play, do something more important instead
    (d) Play to enjoy it but don't worry about the results
    (e) Win, even if you play a dirty game

5   A school performance takes place next week, it is badly under-
    rehearsed. Would you:
    (a) Don't go unless you have to
    (b) Make sure you are seen but slip out in the interval
    (c) Do something else, such things don't interest you
    (d) Avoid a poor performance of something good
    (e) Go and try to enjoy it

6   You have been invited by your housemaster to a formal party.
    Important guests are visiting the school and you are expected to
    give a good impression. Would you:
    (a) Go and try to make polite, intelligent conversation
    (b) Plead another engagement and don't go
    (c) Do something more useful, you couldn't care what
         they feel about the place
    (d) Suggest they have tea with the boys alone, which would be
         more valuable
    (e) Go, but keep in the background.

5 Interviews

We now present the interview schedules which we used with senior staff. For reasons of space the schedules used for other staff and the self administered questionnaires which we used with other teachers have had to be omitted. We do give however one important element of that questionnaire: concerning the roles of staff.

The interviews were all depth ones, focused around predetermined questions but otherwise flexible. We give the areas of sociological analysis of the school to which each question relates.

(i) The headmaster This is a focused interview in depth: It should last anything over two hours. (In some cases it has taken six hours.) Try and get him alone for a long time uninterrupted— e.g. after dinner at the end of your stay. Use each· question as a focus and probe extensively round it. Be prepared to modify or omit questions, to switch the order and to add things which have arisen in the course of your stay—things about this particular school.

Headmasters are busy men but they like to have someone to talk to—stress that this is strictly confidential and be sympathetic. It is quite in order, and indeed usually necessary, to prompt, to quote examples and make comparisons. The more knowledgable you appear, the franker he will be. Pounce on any hints of problems, etc. which appear in answers and pursue them—there are few specific questions on them.

This interview should provide basic material not only on the headmaster's role, but on the school's goals and the official values and provide information and judgements on its organisation as a whole.

Question 1 provides data on the presenting culture, and has implications for goals, roles and values.

	Note
1 Basic data:	Be rather apologetic about this
Date of appointment	—if you can get it from *Who's*
own school	*Who* do so and scrap asking.
university	
subject	
previous appointments	
married etc.—children—	
age—education—career	
wife—education	

Question 2 proves very fruitful. It provides basic data on roles, role conflicts and their resolution and gives insights on organisation, communication and the subunits of the school and their integration. In addition, it throws light on the real goals of the school, patterns of staff association and the relation between the formal and informal orders.

2   I'd like to get a clear idea of Go over whole day from rising
    all the things you do as head- to bed—a great many points
    master of X—could we go should arise here to be probed
    over everything you did on or brought up later.
    a typical working day, say
    yesterday? (Role profile)

Question 3 establishes a role profile of the headmaster, which
is vital to the study of the school or to comparisons between
them. It yields valuable data on the real goals of the school,
on the school and its environment, on the integration of the
school's subunits, on taste and values and staff-pupil interaction
and control.

3   As headmaster you have
    many functions to fulfil what
    would you say your principal
    one is?
    Each of these are dealt with
    subsequently   at   greater
    length. This is to find out
    his more important function,
    and his attitude to them.
    (i) What about *outside the
    school*, public relations (est-
    ablish what he does and how
    he feels about it). What com-
    mittees does he attend, func-
    tions outside school, local,
    national, prep schools.
    (ii) *Administration*: (establish   *Note*
    how basic administration is How much time is devoted to
    organised—e.g. delegated to this.
    others or what they do. Does Communication procedure.
    he deal with admissions? etc.
    Establish attitude).
    (iii) *Teaching* (establish how
    much he does with whom
    and attitude). What subjects.

(iv) *Personal relations* and problems of boys (est. what he does, how these are dealt with in school).

(v) Appointment of staff.

(vi) *Religious functions.* How important are these within and outside the school.

Questions 4 and 5 provide data on role performance, and conflict and resolution.

4   Which of these functions do you enjoy most (probe).

5   Are all these functions compatible. Are there one or two you would rather shed?—explore the four types of role conflict here

Note

4 and 5 can be modified or combined—to get his satisfaction or dissatisfaction with role.

Question 6 gives the headmaster's stated goals. Later he completes the same goals sheet as staff and senior pupils.

6   What are your *broad* objectives as headmaster of X? He can be reminded by mentioning some of the areas covered by goal sheet—academic, social goals

Note

Get his main goals—don't let him become specific till 7.

Question 7 gives further stated and real goals and changes.

7   What have been your more specific, detailed objectives, things you have changed or introduced or things you wanted to change or introduce.

Go over things changed, achieved.

Go over what he still wants to do.

(For this, follow section of sociological summary on change.)

Questions 8 and 9 again touch on real goals and the pressures for and against change, the internal structure of power and communication, and relations with other organisations and the wider society.

8 Did you know much about X school before your appointment?—state of school on arrival—strength and weaknesses—how was he appointed—his relations with governing body—the extent of his authority. Who really takes decisions.

Note
Should elicit (a) different forms of power held by different groups in the school. (b) Methods of communication—vertical ones, e.g. are there staff meetings, can staff know of what goes on in housemasters meetings. Does headmaster address schools as whole ever, etc.

9 How did you construct your policy, find out and decide what to do?

Question 10 explores in more detail the processes of change, the pressures operating on change from within and without the society. The answer is relevant to staff and pupil roles, authority and power.

10 If you want (wanted) to change something, how would (did) you go about it, what are the main obstacles to and processes of change? Housemasters (probe exactly how far he would override the housemasters etc.)
Senior master
Heads of Departments
Bursar
Rest of staff
Boys (consultation with prefects and rest of boys—the extent and nature of this consultation)
Parents

Old boys
Governors
L E A (if applicable)

Question 11 gathers yet further information on roles, the presentation of values, roles, authority and power, the staff informal world and communication.

Note

11 How do you go about recruiting staff?
1 Agencies used
Problems in staffing (subjects etc.)
Qualities looked for—especially social (boarding) qualities
How are Housemasters appointed
Explore the boundaries of Housemaster authority
2 Background of staff, school, experience, academic, sports abilities, who are the powerful staff figures and why. Staff mobility. Division on staff.
3 Consultation with staff. How is this organised—formally—informally

Use this to find out situation re recruiting *and* promotion within the school.

Question 12 provides data on subunits and organisation, value systems, goals.

Note

12 Are you satisfied with:
the academic provision and organisation
the social provision and organisation
(the balance between House and School)
the discipline/Games

Major question—avoid overlap with 7. Get as much as you can.

the boys recruited
size of school: relation
between day-boy/boarders
Fully explore each of these
areas using school summary
as a guide

Questions 13 and 14 relate to the presenting culture, the school and the wider society, reference groups, recruitment.

Note

13 You meet many parents. Why do they think they send their boys here, what do you think X will do for their sons?
intellectually
socially
morally
status-wise
Oxbridge and careers
' need '

Explore the school's relations with parents and attitude to them. Their contacts with school and boys—housemaster relations with parents. Communication with them. Home versus school discipline and values.

14 What criteria do you apply when admitting a boy?
I.Q.
C.E.E.
School affiliations
Prep. reports

Relations with particular preps. or Junior School

L E A entry
Need

The number of need cases in school and seek access to each boy's individual records

Influence of Housemaster on admissions—
How are new boys allocated to houses

Question 15 gives data on relations between formal and informal systems, the underculture, deviance and adaptations.

15 What group(s) or type of   *Note*
    boys come the greatest prob-   Cover some problem areas as in
    lems to you and the staff?   Chaplain interview. Explore
    Why?   Headmaster's pastoral role, and
                                   his attitude to major problems,
                                   smoking, drinking, sex, etc. What
                                   problems must be referred to
                                   him. Can lead to discussion of
                                   school *underlife* official attitudes
                                   or awareness of it.

Question 16 supplies further information on roles and role conflict and goals.

16 What do you personally find
    most satisfying about work-
    ing in a boarding school?

    Are there things you dislike
    about working in a boarding
    school?

Questions 17 and 18 concern goals, stated and real, the school
and the wider society.

                                              Note
17 What is this school really   Get him to make a statement of
    setting out to achieve as far the overall goals of the school
    as the boys are concerned?

18 To what extent is it achieving After general comments get him
    them?   to score the goal sheet

Question 19 reformulates the goals question in another way,
provides valuable data on values and their collective and individual orientation.

                                              Note
19 What particular qualities do More specific than 17. What are
    you like to see in a boy when their best qualities, what are their
    he leaves X?   worst and criteria of school's
                                  success.

20 What do you think a good
    boarding school can do for
    a boy that a good day school
    cannot?

    Add any more questions—
    write them in on your notes.

Also add if relevant
How are school prefects appointed

His relations with the prefects—consultation and communication with them. What do they find most difficult, what are the strengths and weaknesses of the pupils' authority system.

This may be expanded into questions on the informal world—boys' attitudes and expectations—the assimilation of new boys.

In Public Schools question on:
  (i)   The proportion of 'need' cases and attitude to varying sorts of 'need' problems—how does school set out to cope with these.
  (ii) The attitudes to changes envisaged by Commission—admission of a large proportion of children from day maintained backgrounds of a wide ability range: headmasters, governors, staff, parents.
  (iii) Particular problems posed by admission of L E A children on experimental schemes e.g. the Hertfordshire boys at Eton (follow interview schedule of Swindon/Marlborough research schemes).

(ii) The housemaster The housemaster's interview explores the same sociological areas as the headmaster's interview, many of the questions are identical and the cross references to sections of the sociological summary (Part Two) are unnecessary. However, this interview gives many insights into the workings of an important subunit, the house, the relations between formal and informal social orders, particularly questions 2c and i, questions 6, 9, 12 and 13, and much on Authority status and elites.

Try and interview him alone (see his wife separately to establish what she does formally and informally and her attitudes) in his house. This is again a focused interview—get as much as you can by probing. Add anything that seems relevant.

1 *Basic Data*
   Age
   Married (children)
   School (day/bdr.)
   University/degree
   Subject teaches
   Previous appointments
   How long had been in this
   school before appointment as
   Housemaster.

2 Establish the housemaster's
   functions clearly: *Notes*

   (a) Entrants/admission   (Contacts with prep schools:
                               what does he do; how does he
                               select; does he like it, etc.)

   (b) Parents   (What are main points of con-
                               tacts in a pupil's career with his
                               parents; how does housemaster
                               regard parents, etc.)

   (c) Discipline   (Methods, relationship with his
                               prefects—does he delegate—
                               how far, etc.)

(d) Universities/careers   (How onerous does he find univ. placing. Relations with careers master)

(e) Pupil's work   (E.g. to what extent does he supervise it—look at form orders, etc.—what system of supervision is usual)

(f) Games   (How many afternoons does he referee—other activities re games)

(g) Teaching   (What does he teach—how many periods a week—compare general staff averages)

(h) Religion   (Does he take house prayers—involvement of pupils in house religious life—policy on communion)

(i) Personal   (Go into detail with type of personal problems he deals with and other pastoral agencies in the school. Get some idea of his attitude to sex problems in school)

(j) Domestic, other duties   (Appointment of domestic staff, matron, areas of responsibility)

3 Which of the above is most important; why?

4 Are they all really compatible and which suffer from all the rest?   (establish if he has secretarial help. Effect on his teaching).

5 What is the effect of being housemaster on your family and social life?

6   How independent are you as housemaster
    on appointment of house prefects
    on appointment of school prefects

    (Establish degree of his personal independence and that of housemasters collectively, and examine whether duties contractual or normatively defined)

    What are the factors which would influence your selection of:
    (i) House captain
    (ii) House prefects
    (iii) House tutor or assistant staff

    (Explore the extent of their authority)

7   How are housemasters appointed?
    Go over his appointment and the system of promotion—promotion from outside, relations with
    headmaster,
    other housemasters,
    teaching staff
    ancillary staff.

8   How does this house differ from the rest—has it any special characteristics or reputation?

9   What features (social/academic rather than physical—but don't rule those out) of the house at present please you most.
    please you least.

10 What have been the main changes in the school since you came here?
    ones you welcome
    ones you don't welcome

    (Explore here on lines laid down in change section of summary)

11 What changes would you like to see
   academic
   social
   plant
   organisation (e.g. communication procedures)

12 What are the best and worst characteristics of the pupils in this school?

Note

13 Which group or type of pupils offer the greatest problem to you and the staff?
(Assess how much need—how is it met; effects of need on other staff and pupils, and orientation to need)

14 What kind of pupil is not likely to benefit from boarding?

15 What do you think this school is setting out to achieve as a boarding school?

16 What do you think it does achieve?

17 What qualities do you personally like to see in a pupil when he leaves here?

Add if relevant

(i) Day pupils—probe for effect of day pupils and boarders on each other and problems arising from each and their mixture

(ii) Financing of the house—
   how is this organised
   relations with Bursar

Finally: get him to fill in—
   Attitudes sheet
   Goals sheet

(iii) The head of school Objects: to chart the authority system among the pupils and its adjuncts; the status system and the concomitant privileges and insignia of both; to assess the formal and informal groupings among the pupils.

1 Gather some personal data —previous schools, positions held in his prep school— intended career, etc.

2 Go over every office a boy can hold in the school, then in the house, starting from the bottom upwards. For each level in the hierarchy establish
(a) The office held and its duties
(b) How many hold it; how they are appointed, how they are selected—positions of responsibility held up the school. What qualities make a good prefect
(c) Their sanctions (formal and informal)
(d) Their privileges (formal and informal)
(e) Their organisation
(f) Rituals associated with appointment

3 Concentrate on the prefects:
(a) What are their problems, structurally operatively
Notes
(b) What are most difficult (Point out which problems they situations of boys which they hand over to staff) face

(c) Mode of co-ordination (Explore role conflict, the bound-
with lesser (boy) officials aries of their authority)
with staff
with housemaster and headmaster
(d) Degree of formalisation
(minutes? agenda?)
(e) Communication. The relation between the formal
system and informal system.

4 Go over the status and privilege system in the school.
Ascertain status and then the
privileges which adhere to it
(formal and informal). Both
cut across the hierarchies of
office.
Probe resolutely for informal
privileges.

5 Go over the insignia system (Processes of awarding, etc.)
in school
House
Games
informal
formal

6 Ascertain the number, composition and relative weight
of the various groupings
among the pupils, the relations between them.
(a) Formal
school teams,
societies, etc.
(b) Informal
elites
deviant groups
(c) Comments on fagging
system, if relevant.

7 Underlife   *Note*
   (i) Types of deviance   (Communication: Use of sur-
   (ii) The control of deviance names, christian names).
   formal
   informal
   (iii) Permitted relationships:
   Hetero and Homosexual relationships
   formal
   informal.
Get him to fill in goal sheets and attitudes test.

Much of this interview is valuable for the insights it gives to the informal social order of the pupils, key figures in this world are located and can be interviewed, deviants are mentioned, although these usually seek out the observer unaided. Similar interview schedules can be followed for house captains, prefects, etc. and other authority figures in the pupil world.

Similar interview schedules exist for other staff members. For example the senior master will provide all the factual information for pages of the summary. In his interview, information on change, authority, and the staff world can be of great value. The bursar will provide all the financial information, figures, LEA and other support, and the organisation of the subunits.

He can reveal pressures for or opposition to change and throw interesting light on staffing conditions and problems; also give insight into the school's real goals. Similarly with the specific framework of the summary at hand it is possible to interview meaningfully other staff—the games masters on the organisation of this important subsystem, even the domestics and groundsmen can have important roles in the informal system and often act as pastoral agents. However, the interview schedules above provide sufficient illustration of the method employed.

Among the questionnaires and interviews done with staff, the following is of importance. It is a method, using a scoring system by which staff evaluate the elements of their role set. These elements can later be classified so that the balance of instrumental, expressive and organisational roles can be assessed and compared.

The test also explores the principal kinds of role conflict, of time and energy, between holders of similar role sets, and of roles within one person's role set.

(iv) Role sheet Which of the following functions here as house-master/headmaster etc. does the school expect you to fulfil? Score 0-5 according to the degree which the school expects housemaster/headmaster etc. to fulfil these functions.

How important do you personally rank each of the functions as part of your job as housemaster/headmaster, etc. Score 0-5 according to the importance you give each function.

Are any of the following expected of you in your job by the school?	Expected of you by school	Personal valuation of importance
1 Full and active teaching	....	
2 Advising a boy on courses and careers	....	
3 To make a boy socially acceptable	....	
4 Aware of his responsibilities as a future citizen	....	
5 To keep them fit	....	
6 To take a full part in the religious life of the school	....	
7 Provide them with a good example to follow	....	
8 Encourage cultural interest	....	
9 Be always available and understanding when dealing with their problems	....	
10 To encourage a sense of fair play and sportsmanship	....	
11 To make the school feel something like home	....	
12 To encourage them towards self-discipline	....	
13 To make sure the discipline never gets slack	....	
14 Keeping the children fully occupied	....	

15 To make sure they are properly
    housed, fed and clothed   ....

16 Dealing with applications   ....

17 Administering things smoothly   ....

18 To keep up the school's good name
    outside   ....

19 To play a full part outside in family
    and social life   ....

(a) If you do not have sufficient time to do any of these properly
    because of the time you spend on another duty or other
    duties, write down the numbers of those duties which compete
    for time (e.g. 1 teaching and 9 being available) etc.

(b) In many of these duties other people will have similar responsi-
    bilities—functions may overlap. Could you please indicate
    where this is experienced in your position as ....
    (This does not necessarily imply any major clash but includes
    even routine differences which might require consultation.)
    Indicate the duties by the number as above.

                           Numbers
Headmaster   Heads of Depts.
2nd Master   Games masters
Housemasters   Other members of teaching staff
Bursar   Governors
Chaplain   Prefects
Matron   Pupils
Boarding staff   Others
Domestic staff
Admin. staff

    If any of those are major or constantly recurring, please
    ring the numbers.

(c) It is probably impossible for any one individual to fulfil ade-
    quately certain of these roles because they may be inherently
    incompatible with each other. (E.g. a housemaster may find it
    hard to discipline a boy at one minute and to discuss his
    personal problems at the next.)
    Are there any duties which you find tend to be incompatible
    in this way?

(v) Parents An interview schedule was used for the depth interviews with parents. Unlike the previous schedules we have illustrated, this was structured to follow the same areas investigated in the pupils' questionnaire. Some of the questions were identical.

Parents received this attention because the family is the main parasystem in which the child is involved outside school life.

We examined not only the organisation and influence of this parasystem (e.g. parents' perception of goals or participation in school) but cross-checked some of the information gathered from the pupils' writings (e.g. holiday activities qq.44-49) and the questions to the headmaster relevant to the family. It also provides useful material for hypotheses 23, 24, 28, 29, 47, 49, 51, 52, 56, 57, 58, 59, 70-85.

The interview provides invaluable data on the structure, operation, mode of relationships, values and attitudes of parents of day and boarding children. Unfortunately there is not enough space to include the complete interview schedule so the areas covered by the schedule are summarised below:

Questions	Areas covered in parents' interviews	Relevant replies from pupil questionnaire	Relevant replies from interviews
1–2	Basic data about family	31–38	
3–13	Choosing education	20–30, 49, 78	Headmaster, q.3
14–21	Opinions on school	72, 73, 79, 80, 81 84	Headmaster, q.6, 7 Housemaster, q.9, 11, 12
22–23	Contact with school, Opinions of parents and child	50	Headmaster, q.3 Housemaster q.2
24	Goals	1	Headmaster q.17, 18 Housemaster q.15, 16
25–30	Contacts between staff and child	12–13, 68–69	Headmaster q.3 Housemaster q.2
31–33	Opinions on staff	12, 13, 14	Headmaster q.11
34–43	Effects of boarding on child and family	27, 28, 46	Headmaster q.20 Housemaster q.14, 17
44–58	Child's activities in holidays, friendships etc.	41–44, 52, 58	
59–67	Child's relations with family	45–48, 65–67	
68–70	Parents' opinion on child and on boarding	46, 57, 86	Headmaster q.17–20 Housemaster q.15–17
71	Aspirations for child	18, 85, 90	
71–84	Basic data about family, education, income, interests, relations with neighbourhood	39–40, 52	
85	Fees		

6   Scales of institutional control and expressive orientation

These scales seek to measure objectively the degree to which a school seeks to influence various areas of its pupils' lives (see above, p. 91). To concentrate on physical controls and to ignore the less tangible but equally important expressive influence on manners and attitudes would be to ignore a major aspect of the control which schools seek to exercise. There may be a rule that children should not eat in the street, or a sponsored norm that to do so is vulgar: both are controls, and both kinds need examination.

The first scale was devised by listing the most frequent controls over activity, movement, time, social relations and privacy which were found in schools, boarding ones. They were then graded according to incidence, and by the age of pupils and so on. Finally, after much pilot work with staff and pupils, scores were devised to express the felt degree of restrictiveness of each control.

The same procedure was adopted for the scale of expressive orientation but, here, the areas of orientation were limited to sport, religion, leadership and style of life, and the scores generally express the existence or absence of control, not so much its felt degree. More items were included in each area of orientation.

The scores are assigned by researcher after going over each item with several different groups of staff and pupils with much cross-checking between their answers.

Obviously the total scores are not a precise measure of the two kinds of totality but they do enable useful comparisons between schools, particularly if the scores for individual areas are compared, and they enable the level of control to be cross-tabulated with pupils' responses and other variables about the school. The scales relate to hypotheses 12, 18, 23, 38, 40, 43, 44, 60, 67, 82.

(i) Institutional control

A. COMPULSORY ACTIVITIES

1 Is CCF compulsory? (or its equivalent)

Yes for all	Yes for all exc. seniors who have other compulsory activities	No
2	1	0

2a Are games or pioneers compulsory?

	More than 3 afternoons a week	but if choice of major games	1-3 afternoons	if choice	No
for senior pupils	8	4	2	1	0
for other pupils	6	4	2	1	0

2b Is watching games compulsory?

	More than once a week	About once every three weeks	No
for senior pupils	8	5	0
for junior pupils	6	3	0

3 Is the school denominational?

Yes completely	Yes with certain exceptions
2	1

4 Is chapel compulsory?

Twice Sundays once weekdays	Once Sundays once weekdays	Weekday assembly
3	2	1

B. RESTRICTIONS

5 Is uniform compulsory?	All times 3	Some of time 1	No 0	
6 Are haircuts closely standardised?	Closely 3	Within broad limits 1	No 0	
7 How many possessions are boys allowed?	Very few 4	Moderately restricted 2	Unrestricted 0	
7a Money	Pocket money limited and distributed 4	Money distributed only 2	Unlimited 0	
8 Are there locked or lockable storage spaces for each boy's belongings?	None or very few 6	restricted 3	adequate 0	
9 Are boys (other than Prefects) officially allowed to cook or prepare own supplementary food?	No 4	Some are 2	all are 0	

C. MOVEMENT AND ACTIVITY

10 Do boys normally have access to the centre of a town?	No 5	Special occasions 2	Yes 0	
11 How long does it take to get to the nearest large town (not by car)?	More than one hour 4	15 mins to an hour 2	less than 15 mins 0	

12 Do senior boys normally have access outside the school to

	No	Special occasions	Yes
a coffee bars	2	1	0
b eating places	2	1	0
c cinemas	2	1	0
d social clubs	2	1	0
e shops	4	1	0

13 Are boys allowed home for the night during term

No (or only school prefects)	once	more than once
6	3	1

13a Are boys allowed out of the school grounds (or out of close bounds)

	Generally once a week or less	Twice a week	more than twice
senior	8	2	0
junior	4	2	0

b Are boys allowed cycles

	No		Yes
senior	4	—	0
junior	2	—	0

c Are school premises (not house premises) restricted out of class or official activity hours

Severely restricted	Restricted	Little or not restricted
6	4	1

D. SOCIAL RELATIONS

14 Are senior boys officially allowed to meet girl friends out of school in the locality?

No	No but are unofficially tolerated	Yes
10	6	0

Question	Option		Option		Option	
14a Are boys allowed to have friends of own sex locally?	No	8	No but officially tolerated	•6	Yes	0
15 Are junior boys allowed to speak to contemporaries in other houses?	No	10	No but unofficially tolerated	6	Yes	0
16 Can junior boys visit other houses?	No	8	with permission	4	Yes	0
17 Are boys locked up in Houses? summer	before 7 p.m.	10	7–9 p.m.	4	After 9 p.m.	1
winter	before 7 p.m.	6	7–9 p.m.	3	After 9 p.m.	1
18 Are there roll-calls and countings	four or more time a day	4	2–3 times a day	2	once or less	1
19 Are the most junior boys expected to fag	personally & socially	4	only socially	2	never	0

E. TIME

Question	Option		Option		Option	
20 Are most boys over 16 put to bed (autumn and winter terms only)	before 9.30 p.m.	10	9.30–10.30	2	after 10.30	1
21 How many free afternoons are boys below the VIth allowed (excluding Sundays)?	one or less	10	two	2	three or more	1
22 On non-half days how much unsupervised time and unallocated time does the majority of boys have?	two hours or less	8	over 2 hrs. under 3 hrs.	2	3 hrs. or more	0

F. PRIVACY

23 Do most boys live	in day rooms of over 10	studies 3–10	studies 1–2
boys pre-O level	8	5	1
boys post-O level	10	8	1

24 Do most senior boys have separate places for study?	No, work in rooms of over 10	in rooms of 3–10	studies 1–2
	10	4	1

25 Do boys sleep in	unpartitioned dorms of over 10	cubicled dorms or rooms 3–10	single double rooms
pre-O level	5	3	0
post-O level	8	5	0

26a Are baths	open	cubicled	enclosed
	3	1	0

26b Are most lavatories (W.C.s)	unlocked	locked
	4	0

27 Add if the school has day boys:	Yes	No
Does the school expect day boys		
1 to stay to lunch compulsorily	2	0
2 to stay and do Prep there	6	0
3 to stay for evening school	4	0
4 to attend Sunday chapel once or more	8	0
5 to conform to boarders' rules and bounds when at home	8	0
6 to conform to school Prep at home	4	0

DEFINITIONS: INSTITUTIONAL CONTROL SCALE

1 *'Seniors'*: Usually means sixth form (or top two forms if a non-selective school).
 'Compulsory': Means—has to be done unless special exemption granted.
6 *'Closely standardised'*: Use you own observation and judgement: go into the enforcement of hair-cutting.
7 *'Very few'*: e.g. books, pens, pencils, clothes and bicycle.
 'Moderately restricted': Can bring much more—larger wardrobe, other personal possessions, etc.
8 *'Very few'*: e.g. if only a locker for books; *'restricted'* if can store most possessions but not others (e.g. clothes).
14 *'Officially allowed'*: Means is no rule to contrary.
 'Unofficially tolerated': If the practice is discouraged but prohibition not generally enforced.
17 *'Locked up'*: When all boys have to be in House though can go out with permission.
19 *'Personally'*: Do personal tasks for a senior boy.
 'Socially': Do communal chores.
21 *'Free afternoons'*: Afternoons when a boy is free to do as he pleases.
22 *'non half-days'*: Full working days.

(ii) Expressive orientation

GAMES

	More than 3 afternoons	1–3	No
Are games compulsory?			
For Seniors	6	2	3
For other boys	6	2	0
		Yes	No
Is there a choice of major games?		0	2
Are boys expected to watch major games?			
Senior boys		4	0
Others—juniors		2	0
Are any common games formally forbidden e.g. soccer in a Rugger school		1	0
Soccer		2	
Rugger		2	
Boxing		2	
Is the watching of public matches in any sport forbidden		1	0
Soccer		+1	
On TV		1	0
Is support of matches closely controlled e.g. banning of rosettes, rattles, etc— boys expected to cheer etc.		2	0
Are more than 75% of the captains of major sports school prefects or equivalents		4	0
Does headmaster watch important matches		4	0
Does staff watch important matches		2	0
	More than 75%	50–75 %	Less than 50%
Fixture list. Are matches with schools of similar type? (HMC)	4	2	0

	Yes	No
Are colours awarded publicly e.g. in Assembly etc.	2	0
Are house colours awarded publicly	1	0
Are colours worn by boys?	2	0
Are there many on the staff whose distinctions are athletic rather than academic	4	0
Is there an active and significant Old Boys Games group?	2	0

	Most	Just games masters and those interested
Are most staff expected to take part in admin of games?	2	0

RELIGION

	Yes Completely	Yes with certain exceptions	No
Is the school denominational	3	1	0

	Yes	Local cleric takes active interest	No
Has the school its own chaplain or equivalent	2	1	0

	Yes	No
Has school its own chapel	2	0

	Twice Sun once week	Once Sun once week
Is chapel compulsory	3	1

	Yes	No
Is participation insisted on (singing, praying etc.)	1	0
Is regular attendance at communion or equivalent expected	2	0

	More than half	Less than half
How large a proportion of upper sixth have been confirmed or its equivalent (in school)	2	0

	Yes	No
Are boys expected to read lessons	1	0
Are these boys usually prefects or senior boys	1	0
Are boys expected to prepare and contribute to pattern of services, etc. (seniors and juniors)	2	0
Seniors only	1	—
Juniors and seniors	2	—

	Yes all	Some	None
Are the holders of posts of responsibility in the Religious organisation also holders of position of authority outside religious subunit	3	2	0

	Yes	No
Can boys attend places of worship outside the school regularly on Sundays	0	2
Is there an SCM or its equivalent group in school	1	0
Are staff expected to attend religious services	2	0

	Most	Few
Are holders of key staff positions (i.e. housemasters) clerics or hold strong religious convictions	2	0

LEADERSHIP

	Yes	Voluntary in name	No
Is there a compulsory CCF or its equivalent	6	4	0
Is there a person appointed specifically to organise this	4		0

	Yes	as much	No
Have the prefects greater authority and sanctions than junior staff over boys	6	4	0

	Yes	No
Do staff refer or leave boys to prefects for punishment	4	0
Does the school emphasise the expressive roles of its prefects—pastoral, ethical as opposed to organisational duties only	2	0

		Yes	No
Are the prefects to report serious breaches of discipline to staff:			
In organisational areas		2	0
In expressive areas		2	0
Are prefects appointed by			
HM and staff		2	
HM, staff—prefects		3	
By election		4	
•By volunteering		6	
Is there a ceremony witnessed by whole school to mark appointment, do they sign a pledge, receive some extra-ordinary symbol of office.		2	0

STYLE OF LIFE

		Narrow	
Are boys allowed to associate across age divisions			Widely
		2	0
Are boys allowed to associate across house divisions		2	0
		Yes	No
Do boys use Christian names in informal social contact (nicknames)		0	3
Do staff use Christian names in informal social contact	Seniors	0	2
	Juniors	0	1
Do the staff eat meals at boy's tables?	Breakfast	2	0
	Lunch	2	0
	Evening meal	2	0
Do the majority of staff entertain boys informally?		2	0
Is this informal entertainment used to achieve expressive aims		2	0
Is there any attempt by staff to influence accent and terms of phrase used by boys	Junior	2	0
	Senior	4	0
Is the control of personalised space strict?		2	0

		Yes	No
Is the attendance at some leisure activity obligatory for boys	Junior	2	0
	Senior	4	0
Can senior boys watch TV unrestricted in their free time		0	2
Can junior boys watch TV unrestricted in their free time		0	1
Radios	Senior	0	2
	Junior	0	1
Is there an art department		2	0
Is art on the timetable for boys to 'O' level		2	0
Can boys do pottery		2	0
Can boys do metal work		2	0
Can boys do woodwork		2	0
Can boys do printing		2	0
Is there art on display		2	0
Reproductions		2	0
Boys work		2	0

	No	unofficially	Yes
Access to outside world (as D + C)			
Girl friends outside	6	4	0

	Yes	No
Is there any attempt to 'vet' the girls concerned	6	0
Can boys use public transport	0	4
Are boys allowed to have informal relations with domestic staff	0	4
Is there any regular contact with schools of different type. Public with G.S. Sec. Mod. but same sex	0	2
Different sex	0	2

READING MATTER

	Yes	No
Is there a close censorship on school and house libraries	2	0
Are all boys allowed access to Public Library	0	2

	Yes	No
Is there any attempt to control boys' personal reading	4	0
Are school and house newspapers/ magazines selected by		
staff	4	
staff and boys	2	
boys	0	
Is there a close censorship of school/ private magazines	2	0
Is there a formal system for staff/ student discussion	2	0
Drama. Has the school a dramatic society	2	0
Are there regular school plays	2	0
Are there regular house plays	2	0
Can boys visit outside dramatic performances without censorship	0	2
Are there regular visits to theatre	2	0
Music.		
Is music on the timetable until 'O' level	2	0
Is there a master in charge of music alone	2	0
Is there a school musical society	2	0
Has the school a collection of LP records accessible to boys	2	0
Is there an active school orchestra	2	0
Is there a school choir	2	0
Has the school a recognised pop group	0	2
Are individual music lessons encouraged	2	0
Are there regular visits to classical concerts	2	0
Are there regular visits to pop concerts	0	2

Bibliography

We end this manual with an extensive bibliography covering both the section of the sociological framework and the methodology.

References have been made in the text to relevant books and literature. Here is the list in alphabetical order of author. Book titles are in italic, e.g. *The Prison Community*, while titles of articles are enclosed in inverted commas e.g. 'Membership in cliques and achievement'.

P. M. Abell; 'Measurement in sociology' Sociology II 1968. pp. 1–20.

M. C. Albrow; 'The influence of accommodation upon 64 Reading University students' Brit. Jour. Sociol. XVII 1966, p.403–18. 'The sociology of organisations' Brit. Journ. Sociol. XV 1964, p.350–57.

E. A. Allen; 'Attitudes of children and adolescents in school' Edn. Rsch. III 1960–61, p.65–80.

C. Argyris; 'Human behaviour in organisations: one viewpoint' in M. Haire *Modern Organisation Theory*, J. Wiley, New York, 1959, p.115–154.

M. A. Ash; *Who Are The Progressives Now?* Routledge, 1969.

V. Aubert; *Elements of Sociology*, Heinemann, 1968.

M. Banton; *Roles—an introduction to the study of social relations*, Tavistock, London, London, 1965.

R. G. Barker, P. V. Crump; *Big School, Small School* Palo Alto. Calif. Standford U.P. 1963.

R. Barton; *Institutional Neurosis*, John Wright & Sons Ltd., Bristol, 1959.

H. S. Becker; *The Boys in White; student culture in medical school*. University of Chicago Press, Chicago 1961.

H. S. Becker; 'Schools and systems of stratification' in Floud, Halsey and Anderson q.v., p.93–104.

H. S. Becker; 'The teacher in the authority system of the public school'. J. Educ. Sociol. XXVII 1953, p.128–141.

H. S. Becker; 'Problems of inference and proof in participant observation'. Amer. Sociol. Rvw. XXIII 1958, p.652.

H. S. Becker, B. Geer; 'Participant observation and interviewing: a comparison'. Human Organisation XVI 1957, p.28–32 with critique by M. Trow p.33–35.

B. Berger; Adolescence and beyond'. Social Problems X 1963, p.394–408.

B. B. Berk; 'Organisational Goals and inmate organisation'. Amer. Jour. Sociol. LXXI 1966, p.522–534.

G. Bernbaum; 'Educational expansion and the teacher's role', Universities' Quarterly XXI 1967, p.152–166.

G. Bernbaum; Social Change and the Schools. Routledge and Kegan Paul, London, 1967.

B. Bernstein; 'Language and Social Class', Brit. Jour. Sociol. XI 1960, p.271.

B. Bernstein; 'A socio-linguistic approach to learning'. Penguin Survey of the Social Sciences. London 1965.

B. Bernstein; 'Ritual in education'. Philosophical transaction of the Royal Society of London CCLI 1967, p.429–436.

B. Bettelheim; The Informed Heart. Thames & Hudson, London, 1961.

B. Bettelheim; Love is not Enough. Free Press of Glencoe, New York 1950.

B. L. Bible, J. D. McComas; 'Role consensus and teacher effectiveness'. Social Forces XLII, 1963 p.225–233.

B. J. Biddle, E. J. Thomas; Role Theory, Concepts and Research. Wiley 1966.

B. J. Biddle; The Present Status of Role Theory: studies in the role of the Public School Teacher. Missouri, 1961.

C. E. Bidwell; 'Some effects of administrative behaviour, a study in role theory'. Admin. Sci. Quart. II 1957, p.161–181.

T. J. H. Bishop, R. Wilkinson; Winchester and the Public School Elite. Faber, London 1967.

P. M. Blau; The Dynamics of Bureaucracy. Univ. of Chicago Press, 1963.

P. M. Blau & W. R. Scott; Formal Organisations, a Comparative

Approach. Routledge & Kegan Paul, London 1963.

W. A. L. Blyth; *English Primary Education, a sociological description*. (2 vols) Routledge & Kegan Paul, London 1965.

W. A. L. Blyth; 'The sociometric study of children's groups in English schools'. Br. Jour. Educ. Studies VIII 1959–60. p.127–147.

W. A. L. Blyth; 'Sociometry, prefects and peaceful coexistence in a junior school'. Sociological Review VI 1958, p.5–24.

F. Bodman, M. Mackinlay & K. Sykes; 'The social adaptation of Institution children'. Lancet CCLVIII 1950. p.173–176.

T. B. Bottomore; *Elites and Society*. Watts, London 1964.

K. Brill & R. Thomas; *Children in Homes*. Gollancz, London 1964.

G. W. Brown & J. Wing; 'A comparative clinical and social survey of three mental hospitals'. Sociological Review Monograph, 5, 1962.

R. Bullock; 'The coeducational boarding schools' Where XXXIII 1967, p.9–13.

M. Burn; *Mr. Lyward's Answer*. Hamish Hamilton, London 1956.

R. O. Carlson; 'Succession and performance among school superintendents'. Admin. Sci. Quart. VI 1961, p.210–227.

D. S. Cartwright & R. J. Robertson; 'Membership in cliques and achievement'. Am. Jour. Sociol. LXVI 1961, p.441–445.

M. Castle; 'Institutional and non-institutional children at school'. Human Relations VII 1954, p.349–366.

W. Caudill; *The Psychiatric Hospital as a Small Society*. Harvard 1958.

A. V. Cicourel; *Method and Measurement in Sociology*. Free Press, Glencoe 1964.

B. R. Clark; 'Organisational adaptation and precarious values'. Amer. Sociol. Review XXI 1956, p.327–336.

D. Clemmer; *The Prison Community*. Holt, Rinehart and Winston, New York 1958.

R. A. Cloward; 'Social Control in prison' in *Theoretical Studies in the Social Organisation of the Prison*. New York Social Science Research Council 1960, p. 20–48.

R. A. Cloward; 'Illegitimate means, anomic and deviant behaviour' Amer. Sociol. Rvw XXIV 1959, p.164–176.

A. L. Cohen; *Delinquent Boys—the culture of the gang*. Routledge and Kegan Paul, London 1967.

J. S. Coleman; *The Adolescent Society*. Free Press, New York 1961.

J. S. Coleman; 'Academic achievement and the structure of competition', in Floud, Halsey and Anderson q.v., p.367–390.

J. S. Coleman; 'The adolescent sub-culture and academic achievement'. Amer, Jour. Sociol. LXV 1959–60, p.337–347.

C. Coombs; 'Theory and methods of social measurement' in L. Festinger and D. Katz q.v., p.473.

R. G. Corwin; *Sociology of Education*. Appleton, Century Crofts, New York 1963.

C. Coser; *The Functions of Social Conflict*, Routledge & Kegan Paul, London 1956.

H. Craig; 'The teacher's function'. Jour. Educn. Sociology XXXIV 1960.

D. Cressey; *The Prison: studies in institutional organisation and change*. Holt, Rinehart & Winston, New York 1961.

D. Cressey & Krassowski; 'Inmate organisation and anomie in American prisons and Soviet labour camps'. Social Problems V 1957–58, p.217–30.

H. O. Dahlke; *Values in Culture and Classroom; a study in the sociology of the school*. Harper, New York 1958.

R. Dahrendorf; *Class and Class Conflict in Industrial Society*. Routledge & Kegan Paul, London 1959.

R. R. Dale; 'A critical analysis on research on the effects of co-education on academic attainment in Grammar Schools'. Educ. Rsch. IV 1961–62, p.207–217.

R. R. Dale; 'An analysis of research in comparative attainment in Mathematics in single-sex and coeducational maintained grammar schools'. Educ. Rsch. V 1962–63 p.10–15.

R. R. Dale; 'Research on comparative attainment in English in single-sex and coeducational grammar schools'. Educ. Rsch. VI 1963–64, p.170–178.

R. R. Dale; *Mixed or Single-sex Schools*. Routledge, 1969.

R. R. Dale & S. Griffith; *Down Stream: Failure in the Grammar School*. Routledge & Kegan Paul, London 1965.

J. C. Dancy; *Public Schools and the Future*. Faber & Faber, London 1963.

J. C. Daniels; 'The effects of streaming in the Primary School'. Brit. Jour. Educ. Psych XXXI 1961, p.69–78 and XXXI 1961, p.119–127.

H. Davies; *Culture and the Grammar School*. Routledge & Kegan Paul, London 1965.

J. A. M. Davis; 'Secondary schools as communities'. Educ. Review IX 1957, p.179–189.

D. G. Dean; 'Alienation its meaning and measurement'. Amer. Sociol. Rvw. XXVI 1961, p.753–758.

J. P. Dean; 'Participant observation and interviewing' in J. T. Doby, *Introduction to Social Research*, Stackpole Co. Harrisburg 1954.

S. M. Dornbusch; 'The military academy as an assimilation unit'. Soc. Forces XXXIII 1954–55, p.316–321.

J. W. B. Douglas; *The Home and School*. MacGibbon & Kee, London 1964.

R. Dubin; 'Deviant behaviour and social structure: continuities in social theory'. Amer. Sociol. Rvw. XXIV 1959, p. 147–164.

R. Dupan & S. Roth; 'The psychologic development of a group of children brought up in a hospital type residential nursery'. Jour. Pediatrics XLVII 1955, p.124–129.

N. Elias; 'Problems of involvement and detachment'. Brit. Jour. Sociol. VII 1956, p.226–252.

F. Ellkin; 'The soldier's language'. Amer. Jour. Sociol. LI 1946, p.414–422.

A. Etzioni; *A Comparative Analysis of Complex Organisations: on power, involvement and their correlates*. Glencoe Free Press, New York, 1961.

A. Etzioni (ed.); *Complex Organisations: a sociological reader*. Holt, Rinehart & Winston, New York 1961.

K. M. Evans; *Sociometry and Education*. Routledge & Kegan Paul. London 1962.

K. M. Evans; 'Sociometry in schools'. (i) techniques, (ii) application. Educ. Rsch. VI 1963–64; (i) p.50–58; (ii) p.121–128.

R. Farley; *Secondary Modern Discipline*. A. & C. Black, 1960.

L. Festinger, D. Katz; *Research Methods in the Behavioural Sciences*. Holt, Rinehart & Winston, New York 1953.

J. H. Fichter; *Parochial School*. Notre Dame, University of Notre Dame, 1958.

C. E. Fishbourn; 'Teacher role perception in the secondary school'. J. Teacher Educn. XIII 1962.

J. Floud; 'Teaching in the affluent society'. Brit. Jour. Sociol. XIII, p.299–308.

J. Floud, A. H. Halsey & C. A. Anderson; *Education, Economy and Society: a reader in the sociology of education.* Free Press, New York 1961.

C. A. Ford; 'Homosexual practices of institutionalised females'. J. Abnormal and Social Psychology XXIII 1929, p.442–448.

A. G. Frank; 'Administrative role definition and social change'. Human Organisation XXIII 1963–64, p.238–242.

M. F. Friedell; 'Organisations as semi-lattices'. Amer. Sociol. Rvw. XXXII 1967, p.46–53.

N. L. Gage (ed.); *Handbook of Research on Teaching.* Rand McNally 1963.

D. E. M. Gardner, J. E. Gross; *The role of the teacher in the Infant and Nursery School.* Pergamon 1965.

B. J. Georgopolous & A. S. Tannebaum; 'A study of organisational effectiveness'. Amer. Sociol Rvw. XXII 1959. p.534–540.

B. J. Georgopolous & A. S. Tannebaum; 'The distribution of control in organisations'. Soc. Forces XXXVI 1957–58, p.44–50.

J. W. Getzels; 'A psycho-sociological framework for the study of educational administration'. Harvard Educn. Rvw. XXII 1952.

J. W. Getzels & E. G. Guba; 'The structure of roles and role conflict in the teaching situation'. Jour. Educn. Sociol. XXIX 1955.

J. W. Getzels & E. G. Guba; 'Role, role conflict and effectiveness: an empirical study'. Amer. Sociol. Rvw XIX 1954, p.164–175.

R. Giallombardo; *Society of Women.* John Wiley, New York 1966.

A. Giddens; 'Aspects of the social structure of a university hall of residence'. Sociological Review VIII 1960, p.97–108.

E. Goffman; *The Presentation of Self in Everyday Life.* Anchor, New York 1959.

E. Goffman; *Asylums.* Anchor Books, New York 1961.

W. J. Goode; 'A theory of role strain'. Amer. Sociol Rvw XXV 1960, p.483–496.

C. W. Gordon; *The Social System of the High School: a study in the sociology of adolescence.* Free Press, Glencoe 1957.

B. F. Green; 'Attitude Analysis' in G. Lindsey (ed.) *Handbook of Social Psychology* Vol. I, Reading, Mass. 1954.

N. Gross; *Who Runs our Schools?* John Wiley, New York 1958.

N. Gross & R. Herriot; *Staff Leadership in Public Schools.* John Wiley, New York 1965.

N. Gross, W. S. Mason & A. W. MacEachern; *Explorations in Role*

Analysis. John Wiley, New York 1958.

O. Grusky; 'Role conflict in organisations: a study of prison camp officials'. Admin. Sci. Quart. IV 1959, p.452–472.

O. Grusky; 'Organisational Goals and behaviour of informal leaders'. Amer. Jour. Sociol. LXV 1959, p.59–67.

M. Haire; *Modern Organisation Theory.* John Wiley, New York 1959.

J. W. Halliwell; 'A comparison of pupil achievement in graded and non-graded primary classrooms'. J. Exp. Educn. XXXII 1964, p.59–64.

A. W. Halpin; 'The leader behaviour and leadership ideology of educational administrators and aircraft commanders'. Harvard Educn. Rvw. XXV 1955, p.18–32.

A. W. Halpin; *The Leadership Behaviour of School Superintendents.* Columbus, Ohio State University 1956.

P. Hammond; *Sociologists at Work.* Basic Books, New York 1964.

D. H. Hargreaves; *Social Relations in a Secondary School.* Routledge & Kegan Paul, London 1967.

I. Harper; 'The role of the fringer in a state prison for women'. Social Forces XXXI 1952, p.53–60.

M. E. Highfield, A. Pinsent; *A Survey of Rewards and Punishments in Schools.* Newnes Educational Publishing Co., N.F.E.R. London 1952.

A. B. Hollingshead; *Elmtown's Youth.* Free Press, Glencoe 1962.

D. L. Howard; *The English Prisons, their past and their future.* Methuen, London 1960.

E. Hoyle; 'Organisational analysis in the field of education'. Educn. Rsch. VII 1964–65, p.97–114.

H. Hyman; *Survey Design and Analysis.* Free Press, New York 1955.

H. Hyman; *Interviewing in Social Research.* Chicago Univ. Press 1954.

B. Jackson; *Streaming: an Education System in Miniature.* Routledge & Kegan Paul, London 1964.

B. Jackson & D. Marsden; *Education and the Working Class: some general themes raised by the study of 88 working class children in a Northern industrial city.* Institute of Community Studies, London 1962.

P. Jacob; *Changing Values in College.* Harper, New York 1957.

G. E. Jensen; 'The school as a social system'. Education Rsch. Bulletin XXXIII 1954.

I. Johanneson; 'School differentiation and the social adjustment of the pupils'. Educn. Rsch. IV 1961–62, p.133–139.

H. Jones; 'Approved schools—a theoretical model'. Sociological Review Monograph IX 1965, p.99–110.

R. L. Kahn, C. F. Cannell; *The Dynamics of Interviewing*. John Wiley, New York 1957.

G. Kalton; *The Public Schools*. Longmans, London 1966.

D. Katz, R. L. Kahn; *The Social Psychology of Organisations*. John Wiley, New York 1966.

W. F. Koontz; 'A study of achievement as a function of homogeneous grouping'. J. Exp. Educn. XXX 1961–62, p.249–254.

S. Kosofsky & A. Ellis; 'Illegal communications among institutionalised female delinquents'. J. Social Psych. XLVIII 1958, p.155–160.

C. Lacey; 'Some sociological concomitants of academic streaming in a grammar school'. Brit. Jour. Sociol. XVIII 1966, p.245–262.

P. Lambert; 'Interaction between authoritarian and non-authoritarian principals and teachers'. Genet. Psychol. Monog. 1958.

R. J. Lambert; Sociological Introduction to G. Kalton (q.v.)

R. J. Lambert; 'The religious effectiveness of schools', in P. Jebb *Religious Education*. Dartman, Long & Todd 1968.

R. J. Lambert; *The Hothouse Society*. Weidenfeld & Nicolson, London 1969.

R. J. Lambert, J. Hipkin, S. Stagg; *New Wine in Old Bottles*. Bell & Co., London 1968.

H. A. Landsberger; 'Parsons' theory of organisations' in M. Black *The Social Theories of Talcott Parsons*. Prentice Hall 1961, p.214–49.

D. Lawton; *Social Class, Language and Education*. Routledge & Kegan Paul, London 1967.

P. F. Lazarsfeld; 'Evidence and inference in social research' in D. Lerner, *Evidence and Inference*, Free Press, New York, 1959.

F. G. Lennhoff; *Exceptional Children*. Geo. Allen & Unwin, London 1960.

D. J. Levinson; 'Role personality and social structure in the organisational setting'. J. Abnormal and Social Psych. LVIII 1959, p.170–180.

G. Lindsey; *Handbook of Social Psychology*, Addison Wesley, 1954.

S. M. Lipset, M. Trow, J. S. Coleman; Union Democracy (appendix). Free Press. Glencoe 1956.

D. Lockwood; 'Some remarks on the social system'. Brit. Jour. Sociol. VII 1956, p. 134–146.

R. Lynn; 'The relation between educational achievement and school size'. Brit. Jour. Sociol. X 1959, p.129–136.

V. McManus; *Not for Love*. G. Putman, New York 1960.

J. D. R. MacConnell; *Eton: How it Works*. Faber & Faber, London 1967.

E. L. Mack; *The Public School and British Opinion*. Columbia U.P. 1941.

L. M. McCorckle & P. Korn; 'Resocialisation within walls'. Annals of Am. Acad. of Pol. Sci., CCXCIII 1954, p.88–98.

J. G. March & H. A. Simon; *Organisations*. John Wiley, New York 1958.

J. G. March; *Handbook of Organisations*. Rand, McNally Sociology Series, Chicago 1965.

P. L. Masters; *Preparatory Schools Today: some facts and inferences*. Adam & Charles Black, London 1966.

T. Mathiesen; 'The sociology of prisons: problems for future research'. Brit. Jour. Sociol. XVII 1966, p.360–377.

R. Mayntz; 'The study of organisations: a trend report and bibliography'. Current Sociology Vol. XIII No. 3 whole issue 1964.

R. K. Merton; 'The role set: problems in sociological theory'. Br. Jour. Sociol. VIII 1957, p.106–120.

R. K. Merton; 'Social conformity, deviation and opportunity structures: a comment on the contribution of Dubin and Cloward'. Amer. Sociol. Rvw XXIV 1959, p.177–189.

R. K. Merton; *Social Theory and Social Structure*. Free Press, Glencoe 1957.

R. K. Merton, M. Fiske, P. Kendall; *The Focused Interview*. Free Press, New York 1956.

R. K. Merton, A. P. Gray, B. Hockey, H. C. Selvin; *Reader in Bureaucracy*. Free Press, Glencoe 1952.

J. A. Michael; 'High school climate and plans for entering college'. Public Opinion Quart. XXV 1961, p.585–595.

T. W. G. Miller; 'Values in the Comprehensive School; an experimental study'. Univ. of Birmingham Inst. of Education, Educational Monograph, 5, Edinburgh 1961.

W. G. Mollenkopf; 'A study of secondary school characteristics determining attainment in primary schools'. Educn. Test Service Rsch. Bulletin LVI.

W. G. Mollenkopf & D. S. Melville; 'Relationships of school, parent and community characteristics to performance on aptitude and achievement tests'. Amer. Psychol. X.

J. L. Moreno; *The Sociometry Reader.* Free Press, Glencoe 1960.

T. and P. Morris; *Pentonville—a sociological study of an English prison.* Routledge & Kegan Paul, London 1963.

C. A. Moser; *Survey Methods in Social Investigation,* Heinemann, London 1958.

N. Mouzelis; *Organisation and Bureaucracy,* Routledge & Kegan Paul, London 1967.

F. Musgrove; *Family, Education and Society.* Routledge & Kegan Paul, London 1966.

F. Musgrove; 'Parents expectations of the junior school'. Sociological Review IX 1961, p.167–180.

F. Musgrove & P. H. Taylor; 'Teachers' and parents' conception of the teacher's role'. B. J. Ed. Psych. XXXV 1965, p.171–179.

P. W. Musgrave; *Sociology of Education.* Methuen, London 1965.

P. W. Musgrave; *The School as an Organisation,* Macmillan 1968.

T. M. Newcomb; *Personality and Social Change;* attitude formation in a student community. Holt, Rinehart & Winston, New York 1943.

T. Newcomb; 'Student peer group influence' in N. Sandford *College and Character* q.v.

T. M. Newcomb, K. E. Koenig, R. Flacks, D. P. Warwick; *Persistence and Change:* Bennington College and its students after twenty-five years. John Wiley, New York 1967.

P. Nokes; 'Purpose and efficiency in humane social institutions'. Human Rels. XIII 1960 p.141–155.

K. Ollerenshaw; *The Girls' School.* Faber. London 1967.

A. N. Oppenheim; 'Social status and clique formation among grammar school boys'. Brit. Jour. Sociol. VI 1955, p.228–245.

A. N. Oppenheim; *Questionnaire Design and Attitude Movement,* Heinemann 1966.

C. D. Orth; *Social Structure and Learning Climate.* London 1962.

C. E. Osgood, G. J. Suci, P. H. Tannebaum; *The Measurement of Meaning.* Univ. of Urbana Press, Illinois 1957.

T. Parsons; 'Suggestions for a sociological approach to the theory of organisations'. Admin. Sci. Quart. I 1956, p.63–85 and p.225–239.

T. Parsons; 'The school class as a social system; some of its functions in American society', in Floud, Halsey and Anderson, etc., p.434–455.

T. Parsons; 'Age and sex in the social structure of the United States', in *Essays in Sociological Theory*. Free Press, New York 1954.

T. Parsons; 'The Analysis of formal organisations' in Parsons T., *Structure and Process in Modern Societies*. Glencoe Free Press 1960, p.16–96.

T. Parsons; 'Sociological approach to theory of organisations', in Etzioni A. *Complex Organisations: a sociological reader*. Holt, Rinehart & Winston, New York 1961.

T. Parsons; *The Social System*. Free Press, New York 1951.

T. Parsons, E. A. Shils; *Toward a General Theory of Action*. Harvard, 1952.

J. Partridge; *Life in a Secondary Modern School*. Gollancz, London 1966.

A. Passow, M. Goldberg, J. Justman; *The Effects of Ability Grouping*. College Press, Columbia University 1966.

W. Pattinson; 'Streaming in schools' Educn. Rsch. V 1962–63, p.229–235.

S. Payne; *The Art of Asking Questions*, Princeton 1951.

L. I. Pearlin; 'Sources of resistance to change in a mental hospital'. Amer. Jour. Sociol. LXVII 1962, p.325–334.

R. F. Peck; 'Predicting principal's ratings of teacher performance from personality data'. Jour. Educ. Psychol. L 1959.

R. Pedley; *The Comprehensive School*. Penguin. London 1969.

C. Perrow; 'Hospitals: technology, structure and goals', in J. G. March q.v. *Handbook of Organisations*.

D. A. Pidgeon; 'School type differences in ability and attainment'. Educn. Rsch. I 1958–59, p.62–71.

H. W. Polsky; *Cottage Six*. Wiley. New York 1962.

J. J. Preiss & H. J. Erlich; 'An examination of role theory: the case of the state police'. Lincoln: Univ. of Nebraska Press 1966.

Pringle, Kellmer; 'Differences between schools for the maladjusted and ordinary boarding schools'. Brit. Jour. of Educn. Psychol. XXVII 1956–57, p.29–36.

M. Punch; 'The Student Ritual'. New Society. 7th Dec. 1967.

M. Punch; 'A comparative analysis of three boarding schools as complex organisations'. Unpublished M.A. thesis, University of Essex, 1966.

D. Pugh; 'Role activation conflict: a study of industrial inspection'. Amer. Sociol. Rvw. XXXI 1966, p.835–842.

D. Pugh, D. J. Hickson, C. R. Hinings; *Writers on Organisation.* Hutchinson, London 1964.

D. Pugh, D. J. Hickson, C. R. Hinings, *et al*; 'A conceptual scheme for organisational analysis'. Admin. Sci. Quart. VIII 1963, p.289–315.

L. Ridgway, I. Lawton; *Family Grouping in the Infants' School'.* Ward Lock 1965.

G. Rose; *Schools for Young Offenders.* Tavistock, London 1967.

W. G. A. Rudd; 'The effects of streaming: a further contribution'. Educn. Rsch. II 1959–60, p.225–228.

W. G. A. Rudd; 'The psychological effects of streaming by attainment'. B. J. Educ. Psych. XXVIII 1958, p.47–60.

N. Sandford; *College and Character.* J. Wiley 1964.

N. Sandford; *The American College: a psychological and social interpretation of the higher learning.* J. Wiley, New York 1962.

M. Schwarz; 'The uses of sociology in the mental hospital'. Social Problems X 1963, p.219–227.

M. S. Schwarz; 'Social Research in the mental hospital' in A. M. Rose: *Mental Health and Mental Disorder,* a sociological approach. Routledge & Kegan Paul, London 1956, p.190–202.

M. S. Schwarz, C. G. Schwarz; 'Problems in participant observation'. Amer. Jour. Sociol. LX 1955, p.344.

M. Seeman; 'Role conflict and ambivalence in leadership'. Amer. Soc. Rvw. XVIII 1953, p.373–380.

M. Seeman; *Social Status and Leadership: the case of the school executive.* Columbus College of Education, Ohio State Univ. 1960.

M. Seeman; 'On the meaning of alienation'. Amer. Sociol. Rvw. XXIV 1959, p.783–791.

C. Selltiz, M. Jahoda, M. Deutsch, S. W. Cook; *Research Methods in Social Relations.* Methuen 1965.

M. Sherif, C. W. Sherif; *Reference Groups.* Harper and Row. New York 1964.

M. Shipman; *The Sociology of the School*. Longmans, London 1968.

M. Shipman; 'Education and college culture'. Brit. Jour Soc. XVIII 1967, p.425–434.

C. Shrag; 'Leadership among prison inmates'. Amer. Sociol. Rvw. 1954, p.37–42.

R. L. Simpson; 'What is the importance of peer group status at the high school level?' High School Jour. XLII 1952.

R. L. Simpson; 'Vertical and horizontal communication in formal organisations'. Admin Sci. Quart. IV 1959, p.188–196.

R. L. Simpson & W. H. Gulley; 'Goals, environmental pressures and organisational characteristics'. Amer. Sociol. Rvw. XXVII. 1962, p.344–351.

E. A. Smith; *American Youth Culture*. Glencoe Free Press, New York 1962.

S. Soles; 'Teacher role expectations and the internal organisation of secondary schools'. J. Educn. Res. LVII 1964, p.227–238.

B. M. Spinley; *The deprived and privileged*. Routledge & Kegan Paul, London 1953.

M. E. Spiro; *Children of the Kibbutz*. Harvard U.P., Cambridge, Massachussetts 1958.

A. H. Stanton & M. S. Schwarz; *The Mental Hospital*. Basic Books, New York 1954.

F. M. Stevens; *The Living Tradition: the social and educational assumptions of the Grammar School*. Hutchinson, London 1960.

D. Street, C. Vinter, C. Perrow; *Organisations for Treatment*. Free Press, New York 1966.

P. Street, J. H. Powell & J. W. Hamblen; 'Achievement of students and size of schools'. J. Ed. Rsch. LV. 1962, p.261–266.

S. Stouffer; 'An analysis of conflicting social norms'. Amer. Sociol. Rvw. XIV 1949, p.707–717.

S. Stouffer, J. Toby; 'Role conflict and personality' in T. Parsons and E. A. Shils *Towards a General Theory of Action* q.v., p.481–496.

B. Sugarman; 'Youth culture, academic achievement and conformity'. Brit. Jour. Sociol. XVIII 1967, p.151–164.

B. N. Sugarman; 'Social class and values as related to achievement and conduct in school'. Sociological Review XIV 1966, p.287–301.

M. B. Sutherland; 'Coeducation and school attainment'. Br. Jour. Educ. Psych. XXXI 1961, p.158–169.

N. E. Svenson: 'Ability grouping and scholastic achievement'. Educn. Rsch. V 1962–63, p.53–56.

G. Sykes; *Society of captives*. Princeton U.P., 1958.

G. M. Sykes & S. L. Messinger; 'The inmate Social system,' in Grosser, G. H., *et. al.*: *Theoretical studies in the social organisation of the prison*, New York Social Science Research Council 1960, p.5–19.

P. H. Taylor; 'Children's Evaluation of the good teacher'. Brit. Jour. Educ. Psychol. XXXII 1962, p.258–266.

W. Taylor; *The Secondary Modern School*. Faber & Faber, London 1963.

W. Taylor; 'Student culture and residence'. Universities Quarterly XIX 1965, p.331–344.

J. D. Thompson & W. McEwen; 'Organisational goals and environment: goal setting as an interactional process'. Amer. Soc. Rvw. XXIII 1958, p.23–31.

E. P. Torrance: 'Can grouping control social stress in creative activities'. Elementary School Journal LXII 1961-62, p.139–145.

J. P. Twyman & B. J. Biddle; 'Role conflict of public school teachers'. Jour. of Psychology LV 1963, p.183–198.

A. J. Vidich; 'Participant observation and the collection and interpretation of data'. Amer. Jour. Sociol. LX 1955, p.355.

J. Wakeford; *The Strategy of Social Inquiry*. Macmillan, London 1968.

W. Waller; *Sociology of Teaching*. J. Wiley, New York 1932.

D. A. Ward & G. G. Kassebaum; (a) 'Lesbian liaisons'. Transactions I Jan. 1964; (b) 'Homosexuality: a mode of adaptation in a prison for women'. Social Problems XII 1964, p.159–177; (c) *Women's Prison*. Weidenfeld and Nicolson, New York 1965.

C. Washbourne; 'The teacher in the authority system'. Jour. Ed. Soc. XXX 1957.

J. Webb; 'The sociology of a school'. Brit. Jour. Sociol. XIII 1962, p.264–272.

I. Weinberg; *The English Public Schools: the sociology of elite education*. Atherton Press, New York 1967.

L. J. Westwood; 'The role of the teacher'. Educn. Rsch. IX

1966–67, p.21–37 and X 1967–68, p.122–134.

S. Wheeler; 'Socialisation in correctional communities'. Amer. Sociol. Rvw. XXVI 1961, p.697–712.

W. F. Whyte; *Street Corner Society* (appendix) University of Chicago Press 1955.

W. F. Whyte; 'Parson's theory applied to organisations' in M. Black *The Social Theories of Talcott Parsons*. Prentice Hall 1961, p.250–267.

R. Wilkinson; *The Prefects*. Oxford U.P., London 1964.

C. J. Willig; 'Social implications of streaming in the Junior school'. Educn. Rsch. V 1962–63, p.151–154.

B. Wilson; 'The teacher's role'. Brit. Jour. Sociol. XIII 1962, p.15–32.

J. Wilson; *Public Schools and Private Practice*. Geo. Allen & Unwin, London 1962.

J. Wilson, N. Jackson, B. Sugarman; *Moral Education*. Penguin 1967.

N. H. Wilson; 'Grouping in American schools: a survey of research and current practices'. Int. Rvw. of Educn. VI 1960, p.456–467.

J. Wing; 'Institutionalism in mental hospitals'. Brit. Jour of social and clinical Psychology I 1962, p.38–51.

J. Withall; 'Assessment of the social-emotional climates and experiences by a group of seventh grades as they moved from class to class'. Educ. Psychol. Measurement XII 1952.

A. Yates & D. A. Pidgeon; 'The effects of streaming'. Educn. Rsch. II 1959–60, p.65–69.

M. N. Zald; 'Organisational control structures in five correctional institutions'. Amer. Jour. Sociol. LXVIII 1962–63, p.335–345.

H. Zetterberg; *On Theory and Verification in Sociology*. Bedminster Press, New York 1954.

Since this manuscript was prepared, other important texts have been published:

J. Barker-Lunn; *Streaming in the Primary School*. N.F.E.R., 1970.

T. Burns; 'The Comparative Study of Organisations' in V. H. Vroom, *Methods of Organisational Research*. Prentice Hall, 1969.

J. Ford; *Social Class and the Comprehensive School.* Routledge, 1969.

E. Hoyle; ' Organisation Theory and Educational Administration ', in G. Baron and W. Taylor, *Educational Administration and the Social Sciences.* Athlone, 1969.

R. K. and H. Kelsall; *The School Teacher in England and the United States.* Pergamon, 1969.

P. W. Jackson; *Life in the Classroom Unit.* Holt, 1969.

R. King; *Values and Involvement in a Grammar School.* Routledge, 1970.

A. Morrison, D. McIntyre; *Teachers and Teaching.* Penguin, 1969.

F. Musgrove, P. H. Taylor; *Society and the Teacher's Role.* Routledge, 1969.

H. W. Polsky; *The Dynamics of Residential Treatment.* Univ. North Carolina, 1968.

W. Taylor; *Society and the Education of Teachers.* Faber, 1969.

C. M. Turner; ' An organisational analysis of a Secondary Modern School '. Soc. Rvw. XVII, 1969.

J. Wakeford; *The Cloistered Elite.* Macmillan, 1969.

Index